COUNTRY RAILWAYMEN

Country Railwaymen

A notebook of
Engine Drivers Tales

by A.E.Grigg

with drawings by
Alan P. Walker

DAVID ST JOHN THOMAS
DAVID & CHARLES

British Library Cataloguing in Publication Data

Grigg, A. E. (Arthur Edward, *1919–*)
  Country railway: a notebook of engine drivers tales. – 2nd ed
  1. England. Midlands. Railway services, to 1964 stories,
  anecdotes
  I. Title
  385′.09424

  ISBN 0–946537–47–X

FIRST PUBLISHED 1982 by Calypus Books
SECOND EDITION PUBLISHED by
BLANDFORD PRESS 1985
THIRD IMPRESSION 1989

© A. E. GRIGG and A. P. WALKER 1982, 1985, 1989

PUBLISHED BY DAVID ST JOHN THOMAS AND
DISTRIBUTED BY DAVID & CHARLES,
BRUNEL HOUSE, NEWTON ABBOT,
DEVON

PRINTED BY REDWOOD BURN LIMITED
TROWBRIDGE, WILTS.

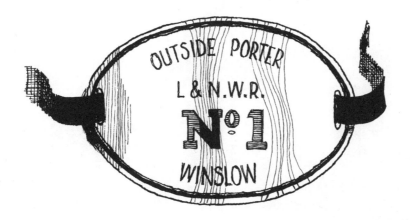

Marston Gate, on the Cheddington – Aylesbury Branch Line
This was the first line to be built off the London and Birmingham Railway:
it was opened in 1839 and closed to passenger traffic in 1953.

Contents

Illustrations

Illustrations

Illustrations

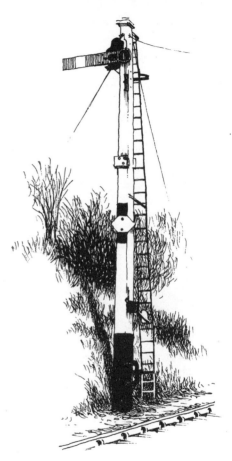

Illustrations

Acknowledgements

For permission to quote from the publications named, we would like to thank:
Bedfordshire Times (1846 and 1874); The Longman Group (Echoes of Old County Life by J.Fowler); also,
Busiprint Ltd (for the use of the drawing of Stowe, from the Buckingham Charity Calender)

For their kind help:
Mrs Sid Sellers; Ben Sawbridge of Castlethorpe; Major Mary Wellman for information about Salvation Army
dress; Reg Waters for information about old railway equipment, and Mrs Waters for the recipe for the Bucks
clanger.

Our special thanks to Hazel Keen from Mursley for her help 'down the line'; M.Minter Taylor, author of
Davington Light Railway, Oakwood Press 1969, for his editing the manuscript, and other friends who gave
their time so generously, Barbara Allison, Reg Howard, Mr & Mrs C.H.Farrar,   and Susan without whose help
we would never have put it all together.

AEG.   APW.

Jim Crow: used for bending
and straightening rails.

Introduction

All history, in the last resort is social history. If we consider the steam engine outside its social context it becomes a dry and barren pursuit. Machines do not procreate: they are machines however you regard them. It is only when we view the old Locomotives in conjunction with those who operated them, do they begin to reveal a character of their own. Many of those who worked the old railways, the drivers, firemen, guards, signalmen, permanent way men, and many others, were countrymen. It has been said of platelayers in particular that, when the railways began, they were the farm workers who jumped over the fence to earn an extra shilling.

   This book is about the working life of country railwaymen, and how they made it possible for the engines to run and haul the trains over our many miles of rural track.

Sam Grigg

Cricket in Metro-land

Verney Junction was the smallest village with a station along the Oxbridge line. It had no dreaming spires or hallowed halls like the cities at the extremities of the line, but because of the lack of these benefits it had a romanticism all of its own.

From when the line and junction opened in 1850—51 until the final passenger train stopped on the last day of 1967, the group of houses which clustered around Verney Junction Station never exceeded thirteen, which included a spacious pub called by the name *The Verney Arms*. There was not a church, chapel or shop in the village; in fact it was not a village, it was just a hamlet which comprised a few houses built, mainly for railwaymen, near to the station which was not erected until 1868. Up to this time this isolated corner of North Buckinghamshire was referred to as Claydon or Winslow Junction.

When the Aylesbury and Buckingham Railway Company opened its line from Aylesbury to this junction on the LNWR, a station was needed and would require a name. The largest landowners in the area were the Duke of Buckingham and Sir Harry Verney who had both played a leading role in promoting the Buckinghamshire Railway and this new Aylesbury line; but Sir Harry owned the land on which the station was to be built so what could be more appropriate than 'Verney Junction'?

Despite a lack of population, Verney Junction was the only intermediate station on the Oxford or Banbury lines to have more than two platforms or an overbridge from one platform to the other. In Edwardian times, when 'the Junction' saw passenger travel, perhaps at its height, it could boast of a bookstall and a regular Thursday excursion to Euston. When the A&B Railway was taken over by the Metropolitan Railway it could also boast that, for a few years before World War I, Pullman cars came from Baker Street to this farthest point in Metro-Land. Right from the hurly-burly of London, for more than 50 miles through peaceful farmlands of Buckinghamshire on the line that was often said to go nowhere, came the two Pullman cars, with their lavishly decorated interiors, bearing the gallant names *Galatea* and *Mayflower*.

Until a station was built at the junction, passengers travelling from the Banbury line to Oxford had to change trains at Winslow. After a wait there, it was on to Islip where the line ended for some time until completion right into Oxford on 20th May 1851. It took one hour by omnibus to travel from Islip into the centre of Oxford.

The Aylesbury and Buckingham Railway Company was established on 6th August 1860 by Act of Parliament which authorised building a line from Aylesbury to Claydon to form a junction with the Bletchley and Oxford line where a junction already existed for Banbury. The Marquis of Chandos (later the Duke of Buckingham) who was the Chairman of the LNWR, now also became Chairman of the new company and contributed £5,000 towards its capital, and his associate, Sir Harry Verney, became the Deputy Chairman.

The contract to build the 12 mile railway was given to Frances Rummens, with Walter Brydone as Engineer. Although work commenced from the Claydon end in February 1861, it was another 7½ years before the line opened. The enforced resignation of the Marquis of Chandos from the board of the LNWR resulted in that company withdrawing from its agreement with the local company. This left the A&B with a line but no rolling stock, or money to buy any, The cost of construction was £67,000 including the building of Verney Junction Station which, although built by the LNWR, had to be paid for by the poor little Aylesbury & Buckingham Railway Company.

The Great Western Railway came to the local railway board's assistance with two new locomotives and three ageing coaches, one for each class, which were formerly the property of the Oxford, Worcester and Wolverhampton Railway.

The GWR thus enabled the A&B Railway to open to the public on 23rd September 1868. Three trains ran daily in each direction with intermediate stops at Quainton Road, Granborough Road and Winslow Road.

The little line was doomed from the beginning and was soon bankrupt. For providing and staffing the trains, the GWR charged over £4 a day, approximately 1s 1½d per mile. After operating costs had been met there was little left of the £700 receipts for the first half year.

For 23 years the GWR were responsible for running the line until the Metropolitan Railway Company purchased it from the A&B for £150,000 and took over on 1st July 1891. The 'Met' immediately started doubling the line and rebuilding the stations. It was not until 1897 that they built a further station, called Waddesdon Manor, for the benefit of Lord Rothschild. They then immediately ran into another problem. The Met had no locomotives light enough to work over the line and they were forced to seek the help of the LNWR who loaned the necessary stock. By 1895 the Met had purchased some new side tank locomotives from Sharp Stewart and Company, two of which were destined for the Aylesbury to Verney line. They had 5ft 3in driving wheels and cylinders, but were not very successful as they suffered from back draught and were subsequently disposed of.

Verney Junction Station Entrance.

21

After a first failure in 1891 a Bill was passed in Parliament during 1893 to connect the Metropolitan with the Manchester, Sheffield and Lincolnshire Railway. On 15th March 1899 the Aylesbury to Quainton Road portion of this line became part of the new trunk route from Marylebone to the Midlands and North, the Great Central Railway.

On 2nd April 1906 the Metropolitan and Great Central Joint Committee assumed responsibility for the new main line between Harrow South Junction and Quainton Road, including what was now the Verney Junction to Quainton Road branch line.

On 4th July 1936 passenger services were withdrawn from Quainton Road to Verney Junction, but the branch remained open for freight traffic. During 1939, work started on singling the line and 28th January 1940 saw this completed. The double line was actually left in from Verney to Winslow Road, the first station but, from a pair of stops near that station, the second line was a long siding from Verney. The level-crossing

Verney Station House and the foot crossing to the cricket field, showing the 'kissing gate'.

gates were then operated by the train crews and all signalling was removed to make the branch one section between the two junctions.

During World War II this single line was quite busy with interchange traffic from the LMS. Coal for Baker Street and the return empties made heavy shunting in the small yard. When the war was over, interchange traffic was sent via the early wartime connection at Shepherd's Furze Farm near Claydon and on to what had become the L&NER for marshalling at Quainton Road, and inevitably the Verney-Quainton line closed for ever. The double line from Verney to Winslow Road remained in place for the storage of condemned rolling stock, but the remainder of the line was lifted in 1957.

The bookstall and Thursday excursion to Euston disappeared long ago, but somehow the station always seemed to have staff that made it a place to remember. A traveller who had to change at Verney Junction could have an experience that would remain in his memory. A well kept station can be an asset to the countryside; Verney *was* an asset to the rural and beautiful Buckinghamshire landscape. There were many summers in which a waiting traveller would pace the platforms and admire mermaids guarding the pool of goldfish. There was the windmill, the seal, stork and elves, all standing passively by, hardly likely to do other than delight any passer-by. A gardener would rejoice in the well trimmed bushes, flowers and lovely standard roses. In the winter time there were compensations at Verney; a small cosy waiting room with a bright fire, shining windows and polished floor, and that window gave a fine view of a wide expanse of countryside.

If we take a period immediately prior to World War II, the duties of the station and yard staff were more varied than those to be found at the biggest London terminus. Jack White was a number taker in 1939 and being a joint station he had to make out Railway Clearing House sheets recording wagons from the LMS lines to the Met and L&NER. There was a considerable amount of London Electricity power station coal routed to Verney via Bletchley and then along these lines to Marylebone. There were then, of course, the return empties for the colliery. The staff brought the trains from the metropolis and performed the shunting in the six-road siding. The Met had its own signalbox, turntable and water column.

Jack was an LMS man so he was concerned only with that company's duties which included cleaning and filling signal lamps, cleaning the station generally, attending to all train arrivals and departures, and

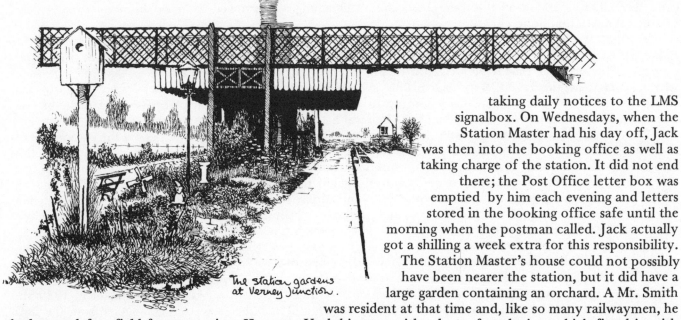

The station gardens at Verney Junction.

taking daily notices to the LMS signalbox. On Wednesdays, when the Station Master had his day off, Jack was then into the booking office as well as taking charge of the station. It did not end there; the Post Office letter box was emptied by him each evening and letters stored in the booking office safe until the morning when the postman called. Jack actually got a shilling a week extra for this responsibility. The Station Master's house could not possibly have been nearer the station, but it did have a large garden containing an orchard. A Mr. Smith was resident at that time and, like so many railwaymen, he had moved far afield for promotion. He was a Yorkshireman with a love of gardening, which fitted in with village life, but another passion linked in even more admirably with the Verney community; cricket was a speciality of Verney Junction. They had their own team and a cricket pitch loaned by Farmer Cowell. Like the station and all the houses, the pitch was along the railway line. When a slogger put a ball on to the railway, there was always loud applause. It was not only the villagers who were spectators, they came from surrounding villages. When Bletchley railwaymen were the visiting team, there would always be a small contingent with them. The village team was more or less made up of the Newmans, Taylors and Cubbages, plus the Station Master. They made an enthusiastic team not forgetting the ladies who made arrangements for the tea. There was also the one and only pub when the game was over. Verney Junction can remember many leisurely cricket days when they enjoyed notoriety for many miles around.

The Bletchley LMS cricket team in the pre World War II years probably centred on George Judge, its captain, and Mr. Tetlow, the Loco Shed Foreman; not that Mr. Tetlow could play cricket but was convenient for the rest of the team to let him think, or openly tell him, he was good. Most of the players were locomen and when a fixture was coming up Tetlow would call in George Judge and ask if he had picked his team. It was known for Tetlow to doubt his own prowess as a cricketer and to ask George if he was really good enough to be in the team. George would quickly assure him that he was indispensable. Then the selected team was scrutinised; if any player in the Loco was on the wrong shift, or if he was on duty in the very early hours of Monday morning, following a Sunday match, Mr. Tetlow was the right chap to give instructions to the Shift Foreman to alter their turns of duty. If several men came on duty at 8am on Monday instead of some unearthly hour just after midnight it was a happy band of cricketers who gave thanks that Tetlow was in the team. The Shift Foreman did not hold him in such high regard; he had to twist other men about to cover the rosters.

If at the last moment the team was short of a player, Tetlow would say 'Where's Dimmock, is he on duty?' If it was affirmed that fitter's mate Ernie Dimmock was on duty then Tetlow would add 'fetch him'. Ernie didn't argue, a game of cricket at Sunday rate of pay suited him.

If Tetlow was clean bowled, someone would always commiserate with him by saying 'hard luck', or something similar, and probably suggest that nobody could have hit the ball that bowled him out. When he was out of earshot, George Judge would then just as likely say, 'he couldn't hit a bloody football'.

Mr. Tetlow was a former Lancashire and Yorkshire Railway Co. man and like so many railwaymen of his time, he had an intense loyalty to his old company so when the little 0—6—0 tender engines off the former L&YR came to Bletchley, Tetlow was probably their only champion. His love of the L&YR was matched by his love of a glass of 'wallop'; couple this with a pleasant afternoon's cricket at Verney with the sojourn to

25

The Verney Arms in the evening and everyone had a very enjoyable day. There was a little snag in their fun . . . the last train from Oxford did not stop at Verney, passing through at about 11pm. One Sunday in particular George Judge knocked up 50 runs and Tetlow and his compatriot Mr. Smith the Station Master, quickly adjourned to *The Verney Arms* and had a line of filled pint pots ready for their teams. Soon everyone was merry and bright and Tetlow was bemoaning the fact that the last train from Oxford did not stop at Verney. When Mr. Smith stated the obvious, 'trains don't run past signals', an idea was born. The signalman was in the next bar so, after a drink or two from Tetlow and his own Station Master, it was agreed to keep the signals on at Verney to stop the last train from Oxford. The merry team and its supporters spread out along the platform so as to make a quick dive into the train as it drew in. Its driver, Jack Warwick, was all smiles; he was often one of the team and no doubt was pleased to assist. But Charlie Cope, the guard, was a different kettle of fish. Charlie was a passenger guard way back in the days when a bandoleer was worn and he gave a dignified wave of the flag at the precise moment. He was tall and blunt speaking and never lost that main line dignity. He took exception to his train being delayed and his protests caused an even longer delay, but he could not stop the merry band boarding the train. On arrival at Bletchley, Mr. Rogers, the Chief Controller was there to meet the train and investigate the trouble. What he met was George Judge boasting of his half century and everyone else delighted with a day of real village cricket. Stopping the train without authority was something that not even Messrs. Tetlow and Smith could indulge in and they were subsequently in trouble with the holy seat of authority at Crewe. There was another match at Verney a few weeks later and Tetlow this time wrote to Crewe in the proper manner and requested the last train from Oxford be especially stopped for the team. The request was granted and the weekly notices published the fact. Everybody knew the last train from Oxford would stop at Verney to pick up passengers.

After another glorious day's cricket and a good session in *The Verney Arms,* the team and its supporters spread out along the platform. The signalman pulled all signals off; there was no point in keeping them on because the driver and guard would have been issued with a notice and a 'special stop' order. But someone had forgotten to issue the driver with this order and he had not read his notices carefully. Around the curve from Claydon came the passenger train drawn by a tank engine travelling bunker first and the driver not being on the platform side tore straight through the station leaving a now not-so-merry band of cricketers watching a fast disappearing tail lamp on its way to Winslow. Luckily an excursion from Oxford to Nuneaton was due by about 11pm and after some negotiating, it was agreed with the Control Office that the train should be stopped at Verney and the merry cricketers put off at Bletchley.

The LMS signalbox had its long-resident characters. Charlie Batsford was a conscientious signalman, so intimately concerned with the running of the branch lines, that he was known as the branch line controller. Charlie really cared about *his* branch line.

Sid Baker had a different approach to life. He had his gun and was regularly around the spinnies and fields indulging in the rabbit trade and pheasants if there were any in shooting distance of the box. He also had a regular clientele of staff in his cabin for a haircut. Many a footplate man, stopped at Verney for a short spell in the sidings or on a freight train backed across the road for a passenger train to pass, would quickly take a chair in the box and, with a towel around his neck, Sid would take snips between pulling levers and answering the telephone, a satisfied customer would be shorn of his locks for a few coppers. Sid also had regular customers in a farmer and his family, but in this case he made visits to the farm.

LONDON & NORTH WESTERN RAILWAY

BEWARE OF THE **TRAINS**

LOOK BOTH UP & DOWN
THE LINE
BEFORE YOU CROSS.

Made of cast iron and
situated on the line side
at all footpath crossings.

Robert Snooks' Lonely Grave

It was 1941 when I first heard of Robert Snooks, a highwayman of lonely Boxmoor around 1801, a long time before the London and Birmingham Railway passed over this desolate spot. I was a fireman on a Bletchley to Euston local passenger train, struggling to keep full pressure steam on a *Prince of Wales* class engine new to me at the time; the shallow firebox and rachet firehole door were giving me some difficulties.

Nevertheless, my driver pointed out two stones about six feet apart, just visible in the grass under a clump of trees way across the field on our right. He said in one sharp sentence 'That's a highwayman's grave'. We were just coasting into what was then called Boxmoor Station and he turned to the job of making a stop with a good fast run-in, releasing the brakes for a quick departure.

In the half minute or so we were standing in the station I heard the beginning of the story of the highwayman. It took two more stations to finish off the story.

Now forty years later sitting in a comfortable seat at the front end of an electric train, I often look across to the lonely grave, which is situated about halfway between the main railway line and the busy road between Hemel Hempstead and Berkhampstead. On a bleak winter's day the knowledge of how Robert Snooks came to be resting there can make it seem a more desolate place than it really is. Snooks cunningly avoided capture for some time, but his ultimate arrest was caused by his own ignorance. It seems he didn't know the difference between a £5 and a £50 note.

One cold and misty morning, in the first year of the new century, a postman on his horse trotting northwards with valuable mail, including a considerable amount of money, was held up near this lonely spot on Boxmoor and forced at the point of a gun to deliver. Robert Snooks made his escape, leaving the empty bags some way off, to be found later by men on their way to work.

The alarm was raised but the nearest postal town was Berkhampstead some three miles further north. A considerable time elapsed before the Postmaster, carrying the rifled mail bags, set out for London on his swiftest horse to hand them over and recount the circumstances to the police.

Meanwhile, the confident highwayman was rapidly covering up his tracks. Berkhampstead was a good 28 miles from London town, so the day was well advanced before the machinery of the law was set in motion. This gave the experienced highwayman such an advantage that as time passed the chances of the money being recovered became more and more remote.

It was not until a very remarkable incident was reported, that the police were able to make some headway. A quiet, unobtrusive lodger at a house in Southwark gave a servant girl a banknote and instructed her to purchase a length of cloth and bring back the change from his £5 note. Unsuspecting she tendered the note to the cloth merchant who, finding its value was not £5 but £50, called her attention to the discrepancy. She returned and told the lodger his mistake. Realising the suspicions he had aroused, he departed hastily leaving no forwarding address.

The number of the £50 note proferred to the merchant proved to be one of those in the postman's bag rifled by the highwayman at Boxmoor. A substantial reward was now offered for the apprehension of Robert Snooks which ultimately resulted in his being given up to the police by an old schoolfriend who recognised him at his home in Kent.

The unlucky highwayman was arrested, tried and condemned to death at Hertford, and it was ordered that he should be hanged in chains at a spot as near as possible to the scene of the crime.

A protest from residents in the neighbourhood got the sentence modified to simple hanging since they did not like the idea of a 'spook' with clanking chains on the nearby moor. The hapless highwayman was brought from Hertford to Boxmoor in a cart; from the tail-board of this vehicle he was launched into eternity.

Robert Snook died bravely without flinching, but he had previously been anxious about his mortal remains and offered an acquaintance his gold watch for funeral rites. The man ignobly refused the highwayman's last request and there was no one to care for the remains. The hangman cut down the body when life was extinct and proceeded to strip it but the landlord of a Berkhampstead hostelry, who was there in the capacity of JP and postmaster, intervened and prevented him from robbing it entirely. The local residents refused to contribute to the cost of a coffin and so his body was thrown into a hole dug beneath the tree on which he had lost his life.

That same day there was a softening of hearts among the burgesses of Hemel Hempstead, who were apparently so shocked by the callousness, they exhumed Snooks' body the next night and reburied it in a coffin which they provided.

The event made such a great impression upon some local residents that for many years bunches of flowers were placed upon the lonely grave.

Robert Snooks has now passed into legend. In 1904 the Boxmoor Trustees erected a simple headstone to mark the last resting place of the highwayman; it was inscribed simply: 'Robert Snooks 11th March 1802'.

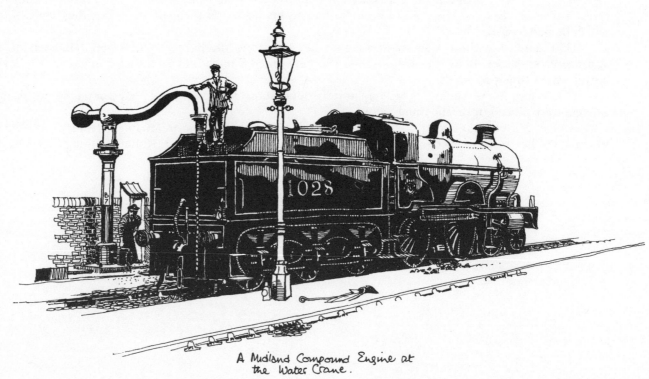

A Midland Compound Engine at
the Water Crane.

Night Train to Cambridge 1941

For railwaymen who worked during the dark hours, the war time blackout provided the moments of greatest irritation: for the footplate men the blackout sheet was a positive torment.

The LNWR engine was the most common locomotive on the Bletchley to Cambridge branch line until after World War II: it was never regarded as the last word in comfort.

Fortunately the time when locomotives were built without a roof was long past, and they were remembered only by the oldest drivers. However the roof tops of the LNWR tender engines offered very little shelter, even when travelling in a forward direction, but when it was travelling tender first the driver and the fireman would get the full blast of rain and wind.

When the wartime blackout regulations came into force, sheets to cover this large open expanse proved more than a problem; it was impossible for either driver or fireman to carry out his job with any real efficiency. Hard, rough tarpaulin sheets were provided, because there was no other way of solving the problem of fire glow without redesigning and rebuilding the cabs of thousands of engines. The sheets were not tailored to fit individual engines, so they were invariably ill-fitting, and probably the cause of more irritation and blasphemy on the railways than any other single object during the war. Because of their size and lack of pliability, they were folded carelessly when not in use, and placed in the front corner of the tender. After a day of being showered with coal dust, rain and steam, they became a sodden lump by evening needing to be wrenched open for use again at dusk.

The unfolded sheet was then tied to hooks on the cab roof. Sometimes the hooks had gone missing and so it would be necessary for the string to be threaded through the vacant rivet holes. There was a similar arrangement on the tender where at intervals the sheet would be lashed to the handrail. Having completed their task the driver and fireman would have imprisoned themselves in the cab, and would avoid leaving it until they had reached their destination, thus saving the tedious job of untying greasy and awkward encrusted knots.

In the summer, it was stifling hot; in the winter, draughts came through the gaps with gale force. Black-out sheets always sagged in the middle, and wet coal dust dripped down the firemen's necks. The taller the fireman, the bigger his problem. Invariably, as he shovelled coal on to the fire, his cap rubbed the sagging sheet and wet particles of coal found their way inside his shirt. Wiping his neck with equally blackened hands was no answer, neither was the wearing of a neckerchief.

When daylight came, the problem of untying the tightened knots was solved by slashing at the string with a knife. It was quick relief and the two black faced enginemen sighed, then bundled the sheet on to the tender with haste as though to say 'we've had enough, the blasted sheet is someone else's worry now!'

It is understandable that a wintry night in the blackout produced little conversation between the driver and fireman and, if a wrong word did escape, a few explosive sentences were the only product of the discourse.

On such a winter's night early in the War, I was a young fireman, with a driver who was in the last few years of a lifetime on the footplate.

Charlie Blane had the typical outlook of the old steam engine driver. Time was time, and if you were running late, an extra bang on the regulator and a few more sparks from the chimney was the obvious answer.

A Prince of Wales Class.

A *Prince of Wales* class engine was taken off a main line local passenger train from Euston in the daylight hours. A dart was rammed into the fire to displace clinker which was already forming; coal was shovelled from the back of the tender to ease the effort during the journey to Cambridge. Then the wet coal-dusted blackout sheet was unravelled and the backbreaking task of fitting it up begun. It was make do and mend as irregular lengths of string tied the heavy sheet to the hooks, or had to be threaded through the holes in the dripping roof.

By now darkness had really descended. The station was eerie in the drizzling rain and inky blackness. The engine was backed on to the waiting train at No. 7 platform; the tender had just been filled with water at the column. Even taking on water produced complications at the start of a night which promised to be a miserable one. The heavy, leather column bag buckled when the water was turned on; it filled out like a solid steel rod, and not a drain of water was passing into the tank. Kicking or jumping on the offending column made no difference. The driver might then move the engine cautiously a few inches to release the buckle. With the operation successful, I left my hiding place and climbed back on to the tender. A few inches too far and the end of the twelve inch diameter bag would have sprung out; its sudden release would have given me not only a good cold soaking but it would have knocked me off the tender, and almost certainly sent me to hospital.

With the fire now well made up and the safety valves showing there was a full head of steam, the guard's whistle would blow and a green light would be waved some distance along the platform which was otherwise deserted. The train was not unduly late; twenty minutes adrift was considered as good as 'on time' in those bleak wartime days. One or two hours for a passenger awaiting a connection was a usual winter time occurrence. 'Is your journey really necessary?' asked the notice outside the station; only a lunatic would take a winter's evening joy-ride to Cambridge!

The wheels slipped on the wet rails and sparks from the chimney leapt into the sky, but with only a few coaches they soon held, and the eerie blacked-out station was left behind. We faced an even blacker forty six miles of rural branch line.

A 'round' boiler *Prince of Wales* class engine was just one more problem on an unpleasant night. The injector steam valve had to be closed just before each stop, otherwise water would get into the brake valve and the brakes would come on, stopping the train, at the beginning of the platform, and resulting in an irritating wait for the vacuum to be recreated before the train could move into the station. I had to reach high on the boiler front to close the injector steam valve, and then take a nine inch step down to close the tender water valve. This was no fun when it had to be repeated at every stop throughout the night. My head would invariably touch the blackout sheet and particles of wet coal dust would slither down my neck each time.

Neither was Charlie enjoying his work. The stations were completely without light; the oil-lit signals were so dim they needed another light to find them, and the absence of identifiable landmarks in the countryside along the line offered the driver little warning to brake and stop in time.

The cross-cut type brake handle was not designed to minimise effort. It was positioned so high in the cab that the driver was unable to apply it without losing sight of the line, which made it even more difficult to stop at a small unlit station with a short platform.

There were few passengers; perhaps a lone serviceman or woman would scuttle quickly out of the train and away into the darkness.

There were brief moments of conversation at the four 'staff' changing signalboxes between Bedford and Sandy. As the signalman at Bedford held up the metal staff, his oil lamp gave a dim background illumination, and I would reach out and grasp the staff as we passed. At Willington and Blunham, the one section 'staff' was changed for another which was finally given up at Sandy from where there were double lines again to Cambridge. In those brief moments of changing 'staffs' one could possibly hear a muttered greeting from the signalman such as 'Hello Charlie' . . . it would seldom be more verbose.

Careering down the Haley Wood bank, the treeless miles of silhouetted market gardens provided an unbroken skyline. The dimly lit signal for Lords Bridge served as the only landmark for the approaching but so far invisible station. The change of sound as the train crossed the bridge over the river Cam told that Cambridge was not far away. When we were into the bay platform of the London and North Eastern station we felt thankful that half the night's work was nearly over.

When the few passengers got off and the parcels were removed, the coaches were pulled away by some unseen shunting engine; then we pulled over to the LMS yard; the not-so princely *Prince of Wales* with her scraggy crew, morose and speechless. There we turned and prepared the engine for its return trip.

The turntable was manually operated. In the drizzling rain it was a difficult and tiring business. The engine had to be set exactly so that it balanced, and with Charlie at one end and myself at the other, operating long handles, we both slipped and heaved until it turned. Then with more slipping and heaving we had to retard the table's momentum in time to stop it precisely in alignment and put the catch on. A few inches too far and we would have to start a new momentum back and risk it over-shooting once againe. Once off the table it was my task to shovel the remaining coal from the back to the front of the tender, and once more a heavy dart was plunged into the fire to loosen a clinker, then with a long clinker shovel I would attempt to throw out the offending lumps. This ungainly weapon was about seven feet in length, and to manoeuvre it under the blackout sheet was difficult beyond description. I would move the shovel backwards and forwards until the piece of red hot clinker somehow dropped through the handrails on to the ground. The frustration was relieved greatly by swearing and cursing. The job had to be done, for without sufficient steam we were likely to have an even more unpleasant return trip.

Kings Parade, Cambridge

With the engine roughly serviced, Charlie made another effort at conversation: 'Are you ready lad?'. I was learning his style and gave a low grunt of affirmation. Charlie opened the regulator and we moved out to couple on to the freight train for Bletchley.

A wet and unhappy guard reminded Charlie that there was a box van loaded with mail for Bedford and he gave the OK to start. With Bedford Station as the only stop on our return Charlie would be able to keep his head under cover for long periods, on the other hand there was some slow running to allow for the exchange of staffs at stations on the single line from Sandy to Bedford No. 2 signal box. Care and concentration were needed to spot the dim oil lit signals, for with a loose coupled unbraked train, they had to be seen as early as possible. Throughout the journey rain still found its way down the driver's neck and the wet tarpaulin blackout sheet continued to shower coal dust and water down my neck each time I stood up after firing the engine.

The 'staff' was finally given up at Bedford No. 2 box which was situated on the edge of the forbiddingly murky Ouse. Each signalman, unrecognisable in the dark, wished us 'goodnight', a farewell which I returned. Charlie had long since stopped uttering such banalities.

Stopping under the wooden canopy at Bedford St. Johns in the early hours, we were met by a small group of postmen, wearing mackintosh coats with upturned collars to protect them from the relentless rain. They had been waiting for our arrival, and our silent misery on the footplate was about to come to an end. One of the postmen, there to unload the mail van, pushed his way under the blackout sheet on to the foot-plate. Immediately he placed himself in front of the open and glowing firehole door; the warmth made him smile and in a jovial manner he turned to us and said with a shiver 'Lousy night'. There was a sullen silence from Charlie. The postman, having satisfied his need for frontal warmth, turned his back to the glowing fire. In a bending position he could see some coal way back in the tender. Intent on pursuing a good-humoured conversation he ventured a question to his silent audience, 'How do you get the coal from right back there?'

Our silent misery came to an end; eight hours of unexpressed irritation boiled over. 'How-the-bloody-hell-do-you-think-we-get-it? it-don't-come-down-by-its-bloody-self! Even the thickest-skinned of individuals would have known he had touched a sore spot. He quickly forsook the warmth of the cab and bowed under the blackout sheet on to the platform and into the night.

I was quietly amused by the incident, and thought it had offered a relief to a miserable trip, but Charlie journeyed on in silence. On reaching Bletchley the train backed into the shunting yard after the remaining mail bags had been unloaded on No. 8 platform. In the darkness the loud voice of the shunter could be heard shouting instructions to the signalman in No. 5 box. 'Four, six and on the shed' bellowed the dark figure holding a pole and hand lamp; it is doubtful if anybody other than the signalman would have under-stood. By a combination of sounds, hand signals and knowledge the signalman in his dimly-lit box knew what was required. The swing of the shunter's lamp, a white then red, the changing of signal levers, and some wagons rolled into No. 4 road and some into No. 6. Then off came the semaphore signal and the engine was away across the main lines on to the Locoshed, and a wet irritating night was nearly over.

The Loco shed gave the appearance that one more engine would burst it at the seams. The endless stream of locomotives over the ashpit throughout the night had come to an end, but they had left the pit almost full of hot clinker and, despite rain and frequent hosing down, it still gave off a red glow in the darkness.

The engine was left on the ashpit. A quick glance at the boiler water level, a hurried screwing on of the handbrake, and the old *Prince* was left to the firedroppers and coalmen.

The rain had stopped as Charlie and I walked down Bletchley Road homeward bound. The shops and front gardens, despite the absence of lights and people, made the early hours seem less dreary. The habit of conversation was about to return: at Brooklands Road as we parted it was a different, more jovial Charlie who said 'Goodnight lad'.

40   Bletchley Station Garden

Sixpennyworth of Coal

The isolated platelayers' cottages between Launton and Bicester could seem, to some cross country railway travellers, to possess a quaint and rustic charm; the quiet rural tranquility of their situation might even be viewed with envy. Clearly there could be no ill-feeling between the inhabitants. Or could there?

Two platelayers, neighbours living in isolated cottages over a quarter of a mile apart, did manage to fall out and the consequences of their quarrel fell heavily on a poor unsuspecting fireman and landed him in a magistrate's court.

It was hardly likely that drivers and firemen who passed the cottages regularly would have any knowledge of the domestic squabbles of those who lived in them. Their knowledge of the lady of one house was no more than that she always waved and smiled as they steamed by.

Farm crossing between Launton and Bicester, near to the site of the old cottage.

41

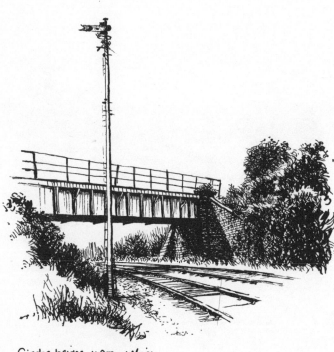

Girder bridge upon which
the policeman stood.

Between the wars, a platelayer and his family lived in each of the two lineside cottages, and the passing freight trains would often push off a lump of coal for the lady of the cottage nearest to Launton. She nearly always appeared at the window to give a friendly wave.

When Johnny Eastaff pushed off a few lumps of coal one day his driver, Herbert Souster, was quite unconcerned, and touched the whistle to acknowledge the lady's appreciative wave. It was not known that the neighbouring platelayer had seen the incident and saw an opportunity to avenge some grudge he had against a fellow platelayer. He immediately reported the incident to the Bicester Station Master who dutifully forwarded the report to Euston.

The railway grapevine soon passed along the message that a fireman had been reported for giving away coal. The official term would certainly not be 'giving'. When other platelayers saw a policeman watching from the bridge carrying the Princes Risborough to Banbury railway over the Oxford line, the news again spread quickly.

Whilst the policeman was still in position, Herbert Souster and Johnny Eastaff stopped at Launton with their train, and with an air of high intrigue, the porter pushed a written message into the driver's hand which said quite plainly that he was being watched and not to push any coal off the footplate.

Needless to say the message was obeyed and all train crews were alerted, but it was a surprised Johnny Eastaff who arrived home a few days later to hear from his agitated wife that a policeman had called to say he had a summons for Mr. Eastaff for stealing coal. Her first reaction to the policeman's remark was to say 'He's never brought any home here'. The summons was not left with Mrs. Eastaff but the policeman returned to hand it to Johnny personally.

Johnny was immediately suspended from duty and had to appear at Bicester Magistrate's Court charged with stealing 28lbs of coal to the value of six pence, and the platelayer's wife was charged with receiving the same 28lbs. However, it was not all plain sailing for the platelayer who reported the incident. When questioned in court about his distance from the scene of the crime, and if he could definitely say it was coal that was pushed off the footplate, he produced some stumbling answers.

The five magistrates were unable to make a unanimous decision on the evidence before them and the Chairman gave the decision in favour of the accused. It may have been incidental to the decision that the lady accused was the daily help at the home of the Chairman.

Johnny Eastaff had his suspension lifted and lost time was paid in full. No doubt he received a regular wave from the lady as he passed, but without a lump of coal accidentally falling from the footplate.

Bicester's Station Master was, like many country SMs, smartly dressed and wore a dignified high fly collar; he was without doubt the source of the grapevine leak and an unwilling participant in the whole affair.

County Police Office and the Magistrates Room, Bicester.

Marsh Gibbon and Poundon Station House.

The Super 'D'

Before telling my story of the Super D engine at Bletchley, a brief history of the 0—8—0 freight engines of the LNWR will serve as useful background, especially when there is no obvious answer to the question 'Why was it called a *Super D?*'.

The LNWR had a traditional design of eight coupled freight engines with a complex history of 30 years evolution. By the early 1890s the need for freight engines heavier than the Ramsbottom and Webb 0—6—0s led to the Company becoming the first British railway to make extensive use of eight coupled locomotives. Altogether 572 were built and over the years there were eleven separate classes; some were new engines and many rebuilt successively from one class to another to an extent unparalleled in British locomotive history. All became intermingled in the LMS numbering system and were finally reduced to three related classes. They became the last LNWR engines in regular service.

F. W. Webb, Chief Mechanical Engineer, is now remembered for his *compound* passenger engines. Compounds were the result of his desire for economy in coal but there were never enough of these locomotives to make much difference to the Company's total consumption, and any saving was probably cancelled out by double heading of passenger trains. The compound freight engines were better, since their reputation for sluggishness was less important. Some lasted until 1928 in their original form.

The first Webb 0—8—0 was numbered 2524 when it appeared in 1892, a simple inside cylinder type. The Joys valve gear and cast iron 4ft 5½in diameter wheels with H section spokes were shared by all the eight coupled classes.

Trials were conducted between Crewe and Stafford to compare the simple and compound 0—8—0s. The compound, a three cylinder (No. 50), worked at a higher pressure and Webb was persuaded of its greater efficiency. Another 110 of these were built between 1893 and 1900, which became known as Class A from 1911 when letter classification was introduced.

Webb turned to four cylinder compound propulsion in 1897 and by 1901 applied this system to heavy freight engines. A total of 170 Class B 0—8—0s were built from 1901—4. These earned the name of 'piano-fronts' because the inside cylinder valve chest cover, which protruded in front of the smoke box, was shaped like a piano keyboard lid, but hinged at the bottom.

George Whale succeeded Webb in 1903 and his main preoccupation was the

The Super D.

replacement or rebuilding of the compound passenger engine. From then, rebuilds of the various 0—8—0s became Classes A, B, C, C1, or D. The D Class was a great success and to the end of LNWR steam, products of the later superheated development of this class were known to all enginemen as the Super Ds.

Whale also did some rebuilding of the B Class and his first attempt at improving them was by turning 36 of these into 2—8—0s between 1904—8; these became Class E, and two were developed still further, becoming Class F.

Development of the 0—8—0 continued. Bowen-Cooke succeeded Whale in 1909 and his most important contribution to the LNWR stock was superheating.

In 1912 of the new G Class, No. 2653 was fitted with a Schmidt superheater and extended smokebox, becoming the G1 prototype. Large numbers of the G1 Class were ordered between 1912—18, 170 being turned out at Crewe in those years.

Beames was Bowen-Cooke's successor and he introduced the final development of the Crewe 0—8—0s by raising the boiler pressure of superheated engines to 175 p.s.i.

There were also G2 and G2A Classes but for some reason the *D* was remembered most often as the class letter for the 0—8—0 freight engines and it became the most familiar of the LNWR locomotives.

At Bletchley these engines will long be remembered, not only because they were the last LNWR engines at the depot, but also because they will always be associated with heavy brick and chalk trains and, of course, the World War 2 troop trains which ran between Oxford and Cambridge.

Up to 1923 all eight coupled engines had been fitted with round top fireboxes, but in 1924 a new standard superheated boiler with a Belpaire firebox was introduced which could be used on either G1 or G2 Classes.

It was in 1914 that vacuum brakes were adopted as standard and a cylinder located under the cab. The brake was not as good as could be desired and from May onwards many were fitted with a second cylinder between the frames in front of the cab. This cylinder operated the brakes on the two leading axles, the original cylinder operating the rear two. The tender also had a brake cylinder.

In the course of these years an unofficial practice grew amongst the drivers of loose-coupled freight trains to release the vacuum brake on both sides of the cylinders so that it could not be applied automatically, thereby saving steam, brake-drag and the noise of the ejector when running.

This malpractice developed into quite a skilful art and a description of its operation will not come amiss, neither will a personal account of an incident where it truly misfired.

The Webb standard cross-cut brake handles were fitted to the Super D. To create, or 'blow up' the vacuum in the cylinders, the handle was pushed across not quite to its limit, and the handle was duplicated so that it could be used on either side of the cab. The remainder of the cross movement, when needed, enabled the ejector to create a vacuum on the reservoir side of the brake cylinders only. This ensured that the brakes would not leak off. The Duplex vacuum gauge was on the cab side just above the driver's head as he sat on the half-moon wooden seat. Below the gauge, the brass rose valve was convenient to open and destroy the vacuum in the reservoir side of the brake cylinders when it was desired to run without the automatic vacuum brake on the engine.

When the driver was ready to depart with a loose-coupled train, and with a good run in front of him, the rose valve was unscrewed with the brake applied and the reservoir side of the brake would be released. During the train journey, control was kept by easing the regulator according to the line gradient. Some use would be made of the tender handbrake, but often the journey could be completed without the use of the vacuum brake until arrival at the destination. Often the possibility of rolling just a little beyond the stop signal could be averted by reversing the engine and gently opening the regulator to come, perhaps a little abruptly, to a stand.

It all worked very well and, if the train looked like getting out of control the driver could create a vacuum in reasonable time, or push the brake handle right over to produce a vacuum on the reservoir side of the cylinders, gradually applying his brake according to his needs. But it was known to fail and I had the enlightening experience of once watching my driver break into a sweat when the unexpected happened.

The Banbury to Swanbourne sidings local freight had jogged its way across the single line, changing the 'staff' three times, coming out on the double line at Verney Junction. While waiting briefly at the junction the driver, Wally Cox, released his brake on the Super D No. 9005 to travel the up gradient past Swanbourne Station. He then had to recreate his vacuum and apply the brakes to roll gently down hill into Swanbourne marshalling yard. We would then return, light engine, to Bletchley shed and home.

It was quite a heavy train on this occasion with a mixture of empty wagons, a few box vans and some loaded ironstone wagons on the rear of the train. It was also a very heavy pull through Winslow and Swanbourne Station but with plenty of steam there would be no problems. Over the summit, Wally shut the regulator and the train began coasting down the bank. It was then he pushed the brake handle right across to create a vacuum on the reservoir side but within seconds it was obviously not going to work. There was no undue concern at this stage, and Wally pulled his brake handle right back to create a vacuum on the train pipe and reservoir, before destroying the train pipe vacuum and applying the brake. It was soon obvious that this would not create the vacuum either, and the heavy stone on the rear was by now taking over and the train was going unchecked down the bank. 'HANDBRAKE' shouted Wally and I frantically turned the tender handbrake wheel and, with one foot on the tender for leverage, I screwed it on as hard as I could. Wally was now desperately pushing the brake handle backwards and forwards as though unable to believe it could happen. A few seconds of useless effort and Wally turned to his only alternative. Into back gear went the reversing wheel but the old D refused with an unholy groan. A very alarmed driver feverishly turned the wheel forward again but, with the increasing speed of the train, it was now kill or cure. He returned to back gear, and gradually opened the regulator.

The Super D was not intended to be that super. I stood helplessly on the fireman's side watching Wally opening and closing the regulator in a frantic effort to halt the train's runaway flight; the sheer weight of the train was rapidly taking control on a down gradient.

It was then the old D seemed as though it could take the punishment no longer and in its protest, a blue pungent smoke rose from beneath the reversing gear wheel. I caught sight of small pieces of the Joys valve gear shooting out from under the boiler, over the framing, on to the permanent way and then the groaning engine relapsed into a monotonous clanking.

The home signal at Swanbourne sidings remained defiantly in the on position as Wally incessantly blew the engine whistle.

In the adjoining shunting

Swanbourne Station: the farm behind the fence to the left supplied the Royal Household with milk during the time of Queen Victoria.

49

neck the shunter stood open mouthed wondering and watching as Wally shouted 'I CAN'T STOP, I CAN'T STOP'. In the four foot, two signal linesmen straightened their backs whilst examining the signal locking, then realising the oncoming train was not going to stop, casually stepped clear. It was just as the engine passed over the signal locking that the big-end dropped down. My stomach heaved as the engine gave a distinct lift but quickly settled. The two signalmen scooted up to the safety of the lineside bank to watch us career towards Bletchley.

It was onward ever onward, but fortunately the guard having perceived that we were not making our booked call at Swanbourne sidings, applied his handbrake, and with the tender brake hard on, the runaway D gradually slowed down as though exhausted. Near Flettons signalbox, less than half a mile from the main line junction, the quiet broken LNWR 0—8—0, with two amazed crew aboard, stood and awaited the breakdown train.

What had been the cause of it all? If memory serves me right the rear vacuum pipe had come off the stopper, and the brake would not create a vacuum on the reservoir side of the cylinders when the brake handle was pushed right across. We were so busy counting our blessings at the time that neither of us looked for the cause. If the points at Swanbourne sidings had been set for the yard, as was our booked route, it would have been a far different story. The train would have careered through one of the reception roads and providing it was empty, right down to the stops at the far end of the yard. The short sand drag would have had little effect on our progress, and the buffer stops would have been wrecked under the weight of the engine and train . . . beyond, there was a drop and a field at a considerably lower level; *that* would have been the resting place of a not-so-super Super D.

In a Country Churchyard

Castlethorpe has no special claim to railway distinction. Today it does not even possess a station, although four busy lines do run close by the village. When Robert Stephenson completed the London and Birmingham Railway in 1838, Castlethorpe was considered too insignificant to be given a station. However, there was a change of heart and in 1882 one was built, and remained open until 1964. In that time the village produced not only its railway characters but a great deal of milk as well! If you have not heard of the Castlethorpe Milk Train or Ben Sawbridge or Farmer Amos, it is time the story was told.

Castlethorpe is still a pleasant village with a variety of attractive brick buildings which blend well with the older stone houses and thatched cottages. A couple of shops, one pub and a small church in a dominant position, together with the higgledy-piggledy array of houses, all cluster to the side of the railway. Four lines pass through from Euston to the far north, but Castlethorpe no longer benefits since the trains have ceased to stop there. Even

51

The Church of St Simon St Jude
Castlethorpe.

The Station Master's House,
Castlethorpe.

The Carrington Arms,
Castlethorpe.

their familiar rhythmic clatter has changed since overhead electrification and the introduction of the long welded rail.

The station was conveniently near the village. The Station Master's house, built in a mixture of Staffordshire blue and local brick, stood on the west bank close to the platforms. The high signal box, a village landmark for many years, has now been demolished. It stood so near the road bridge it was said the signal man could shake hands with passers-by. Other important features for enginemen in the days of steam were, of course, the water troughs which lay about a quarter of a mile south of the station. Although these have long been removed, the dilapidated water-softening tank remains and the water reservoir on the opposite side of the railway, always attractively camouflaged by trees and bushes, is now well overgrown.

The former station sidings are now an unkempt area; it once comprised two roads, a cattledock, a shunting neck leading from the slow lines, and held timber, cattle, sugar beet, and local coalmen's wagons. Daily the wagons were shunted by the station's best remembered train— the Castle-thorpe Milk.

In the early hours of the morning, before and during World War II, an LNWR Cauliflower would creep from Bletchley Loco Shed, and depart at 5.10 am with wagons for Castlethorpe.

Six miles north a few wagons would be detached for

The high signal box, Castlethorpe

53

Wolverton yard and an empty van would then be placed in the Newport bay to be attached to the motor train for Newport Pagnell milk. Northward again for about three miles and Castlethorpe was reached; the end of the journey. The two roads were shunted, wagons placed for traders and the milk loaded. At 8.26 am the milk train departed. With the engine now facing south, a dip at the troughs would fill the tender tank, and then there was the stop at Wolverton to attach the Newport Pagnell milk van before the journey could be resumed.

On the return trip the train would be backed inside Loughton's single siding for more milk to be loaded. A blast on the whistle whilst reversing often made late arrivals flick the reins to make their horses trot the last few yards down the slope towards the milk stage. This rural spot is now the site of the new station of Central Milton Keynes, the heart of the New City.

Arrival at Bletchley saw the milk vans joined with others from Oxford, Banbury and Cambridge branch lines. These formed the London train; soon the milk would be on the tables of those living in the great metropolis.

I remember my first associations with the Castlethorpe Milk. I was a young fireman, and the time was 2.00 am on a winter's morning during World War II: the 'Little 18 inch' was the name the Bletchley enginemen gave the Webb Cauliflower. The coalman had diligently over-filled the tender and the coal had rolled down to cover the footplate. Heavy snow weighed down the middle of the blackout sheet so far that it actually touched the coal on the footplate. The only way I was able to enter the cab was on hands and knees; then by raising on all fours I lifted the sodden sheet with my back and off-loaded the snow into the tender. I managed to improve conditions further by shovelling coal straight from the floor into the firebox until I was finally able to see the footplate!

The arrival of my driver did not herald tidings of great joy. He was an old top-link driver with a heavy moustache and a three inch pipe in his mouth which was seldom alight despite his apparent unlimited supply of matches; his greeting was little more than a grunt. I oiled the underneath motion of the engine as we prepared it for the day's work. Soon the driver reached his usual disposition of silence, punctuated by grunts to intimate his wishes. The trip was made tender first; amid open snow covered fields, we had to face an ice cold blast all the way to Castlethorpe. The return trip, engine first seemed a comparative joy-ride.

I revisited Castlethorpe on a pleasant spring day in 1978. It was pleasing to have such memories then, but I was soon distracted. I noticed a stained glass window in the church. In the high window, numerous small leaded panes symbolized the history of Castlethorpe. The main coloured figures were of a military man in armour, with a sword, matched with two pious gentlemen who also carried swords . Between them stood the wooden castle — destroyed in Cromwell's time — which gave the village its name. Beneath, three stonemasons also played a part in the scene.

Below the large figures, in separate small panes of glass, were two easily recognisable scenes of Castle-thorpe. One depicted a ploughman with two shire horses turning the soil and in the distance, a spire, probably that of nearby Hanslope Church: the other portrayed a LNWR 0—6—2 coal tank engine No. 973, with the two enginemen clearly performing their everyday task.

My curiosity, to see the window from the interior of the church, was thwarted by a locked door, but a gardener opposite the church help-fully suggested I should 'See Ben Sawbridge at the Post Office just 'round the corner there'.

The well stocked general store was doing a steady weekend trade but whilst Mrs. Sawbridge was serving postal orders and vegetables, Ben, in his relaxed country clothes and water boots, regarded my request with enthusiasm. Within minutes we were in his Morris 1000 to drive the few hundred yards, through the church gateway and into the quiet churchyard.

He was no ordinary member of the com-munity; for there was more to life than just the Post Office and the general store. Ben was the

Castlethorpe Station

village postman, parish councillor, school governor, churchwarden and perhaps most demanding of all, he was village undertaker with some good cheap rates to offer. He could quote several long distance jobs to prove he was very competitive!

To have become such a central figure in the village Ben first learned the trade of carpenter in the Railway Carriage Works at Wolverton, but with a desire to be his own boss, he left the works to become a porter at Castlethorpe Station; well situated to build up his own business interests until such time he could leave railway service.

While I talked to Ben I remembered a Sunday evening in 1964 when I was at Castlethorpe with several others to witness the last passenger train to stop there. The prospective Labour MP and his followers were also there to give rousing speeches on the village green about the closures. This was followed by a token protest by some who, for a while, sat in front of the train before it finally departed carrying a contingent who proposed to hand a petition to the Minister of Transport. Among those left behind on the slow line platform was Farmer Amos.

Farmer Amos, true to his Christian name, was a local farmer and he well remembered seeing the arrival and departure of the *first* passenger train at Castlethorpe Station during August 1882. Now he stood quietly watching the last.

I asked Ben if Farmer Amos was still alive. 'Oh, I boxed him up and buried him over there, with his hob-nailed boots on, at the age of 96'. Ben indicated a weathered stone near the church side gate, adding that Farmer Amos had especially requested that he should be buried in his boots, and that he should be carried in the hearse to the church by a circuitous route via Cosgrove to be met there by his sons. Ben had carried out his wishes and Farmer Amos now rested in Castlethorpe churchyard with other long departed members of his family.

Across the fields and coming into view the new city spreads and pushes its way towards Castlethorpe, quiet as ever and slow to change. Will it be subjected to Town Planning, and forced to take the doubtful advantages of modern suburbia? To me Castlethorpe will always be synonymous with milk and the little Cauliflower engine that regularly disturbed the morning calm as it met the early milk carts that trundled through the village from the farms.

Farmer Amos and friends

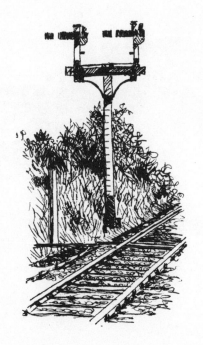

Wolverton's Junior Porter of 1922

Sid Sellers started work on the railways in 1917 at the age of 14 and this was his first promotion. It was a position to be proud of, Junior Porter at Wolverton in 1922. Fully instructed in his new duties, and with LNWR buttons shining on his new uniform, he was on the threshold of a long railway career. *The Premier Line* had well established traditions, and there were strict rules concerning dress. Black shoes or boots were compulsory, also a black tie, which was little more than a slender ribbon to fit the narrow white collar. "Why a *black* tie? asked the smart 19 year old porter: he was told very quickly and proudly by his elders that a black tie became regulation dress for the mourning of Queen Victoria, and the rule was still in force.

Although his home was only seven miles away, Sid was required to lodge locally but he was paid no allowance for this extra expense and inconvenience. He was fortunate in taking the lodgings of his predecessor which were shared with an elder colleague. His predecessor had been transferred to Bletchley for the sound economic reason that at 28 years of age he could not expect to draw adult wages and perform duties which were classified as only 'junior', and so, Sid Sellers was installed in his Wolverton lodgings at twenty two shillings a week, with a weekly wage of fifteen shillings plus 12/6 war bonus. Sid was on the ladder to Signalman —Special Class.

The station was the third to be built at Wolverton, and it brought about a rearrangement of the railway and its sidings. The former main line, running through the Carriage Works, was moved eastwards from the Blue Ridge rejoining its original path at the viaduct over the Ouse Valley. This alteration, often called 'Moons Folly' resulted in a curve on the main lines through the station, which put a cant on the rails that tilted high speed trains and gave them a ghostly presence, especially to the cautious platelayers working at either end of the station.

The wooden station frontage was neat and plain but not without elegance, unlike the facades of many Victorian stations of greater importance. The first station has been described by contemporary historians as one of the wonders of the world; the architect of this station had settled for practical charm. In 1922 41 years after its re-opening the station had a four mile branch line to Newport Pagnell also, it served a railway carriage works that could justifiably boast of building some of the finest coaching stock in the world. The Workmen's morning 'special' from Newport Pagnell hardly came into that category. It was old stock, painted brown and lit by gas. The six coaches were stabled at Newport Pagnell overnight and in the morning were attached to the ordinary two or three coach train and taken to Wolverton. There they remained during the day until used for the return journey in the evening. It was the junior porter's duty to light the gas by turning a tap at the end of each carriage and then taking a precarious walk along the roofs of the coaches, lighting each jet by opening a small lid on each roof and inserting a special pilot lamp. There was a concession to safe working; in icy or very frosty weather he was not allowed to undertake his perilous stroll!

The workmen were aware of this instruction and many came prepared with a candle on cold mornings. As the train departed, candles could be seen burning with pairs of cupped hands around the flames for warmth. The Bletchley Workmen's train had the comparative luxury of gas, which was lit automatically from the end of each coach. There was a specially adapted wagon containing two large gas cylinders. The gas came from the railway company's own gas works situated just north of the station.

Perhaps unique on the railways at that time, the signals at Wolverton Station were lit by gas, two exceptions being the distant up and down signals, which were lit by oil. It was the junior porter's duty to turn on the gas lit signal just before dusk and off again in the morning. In the summer, he had to book on earlier to turn off the gas thereby saving money. Junior porter Sid Sellers did on one occasion fail to

Wolverton Station: the 'stops' are where the Newport trains once arrived.

turn on the signal lights until well after dark. The expresses roared through the station: only the distant signals were alight and they were in the off position. Fortunately nothing untoward occurred.

Each day Sid had to climb to the top of the very high distant signals to refill the lamps with paraffin. The up distant signals were on the viaduct and the Ouse Valley below looked a long way down and very manacing. The down distant signals were a mile away from the lamp room which was under the station. It was a blessing when eight day lamps came into use a few years later. The lamp room was always regarded as the porter's room; it sported a shove ha'penny board which had been there since the station was built.

Eighty years or so earlier the first Wolverton Station had been renowned for its two refreshment rooms. Then, all trains stopped at Wolverton to change engines. In 1922 the only special facility for travellers, apart from two very modest waiting rooms was a large bookstall between platforms 4 and 5.

There was a lot of activity around the station during the day as many expresses, passenger and freight, passed through. The Wolverton to Stony Stratford steam tram had its terminus outside the station. On a special extension of the line inside, the tram took on a wagon of coke which it delivered to the tram depot at Stony Stratford.

A daily arrival in the Newport Bay was an old coach called the 'Rag Cart' which the porters loaded with material consigned for the works. Lamps, vacuum pipes, station furniture and barrows in need of repair came from stations all over the LNWR system. Old iron footwarmers, long out of use, were still being found and returned as scrap.

Visits by commercial travellers with their large skips of wares provided special work for the station porter. To take the skip by barrow to a shop in the town and return for it at about 5 pm was worth a one or two shilling tip!

The Steam Tram from Stony Stratford to Wolverton Station: closed after the General Strike 1926.

On market day, a van load of goods would be detached from the rear of a passenger train from Northampton and placed in the Newport Bay. It was a Friday ritual for the porters to unload the van and take the goods by barrow up to street level using the station's hydraulic lift. There, local traders would remove their produce to market.

A contractor with his own horse and cart was available to deliver goods into the town, and he resented private enterprise on the part of Wolverton's junior porter especially when it involved the lucrative removal of commercial travellers' skips.

In the station yard, cattle were often loaded and unloaded. On one occasion Sid Sellers loaded some beasts and labelled the wagon accordingly. The train had reached Blisworth, only 12 miles away, when a cow began to calve. The cattle wagon had to be detached to allow the cow to complete its labour which, of course, resulted in a delay. As it was so near to the departure point, Sid was in trouble and told that in future he must get the farmer to sign to say no cow would calve en route. When the next consignment was due to leave, Sid asked the farmer to sign the statement. 'I'm not signing that, you bloody fool,' he said. 'Why not?' asked Sid, innocently 'Because they're Bullocks!' Sid continued to request farmers' signatures without success.

When the station gong sounded five times at 1.20 pm the porter knew the mixed train from Newport Pagnell was about to arrive and this provided Sid with yet one more job. When it came to a stand just outside the station he had to uncouple the goods part of the train. The passenger train would then draw into the station and the shunt engine would couple up to the goods wagons, drawing them into the middle road. Sid would then accompany them to the south sidings and work the points from the frame at the subway to allow the wagons to proceed under the fast lines into the goods yard.

A similar job would occur when royal coaches needed to be turned on the Newport angle. This time Sid took the single line 'staff' from the Newport engine while it waited in the station, and accompanied the locomotive and royal coaches along the Newport line to the Bradwell Curve where he unlocked the points with the 'Staff' to enable the train to go round the angle.

The junior porter could always fill uneventful moments with routine work about the station. The platforms had to be swept and all the toilets cleaned. There were no short cuts in this latter task since Mrs. Kemp, the ladies' lavatory inspector paid spot visits to keep an eye on the little room prominently marked *Ladies.* However, for Sid Sellers, it was not quite 'routine' on one distressing and unforgetable occasion. Seeking the reason for an unpleasant odour that had been coming from the ladies' waiting room for a number of days, he turned up the lid of the large coal fired stove and, pulling out a bundle of newspapers, discovered the decomposing body of a six week old baby, this was an appalling occurrence especially for a small country town in the early 20's, and Wolverton was profoundly shocked by it.

The station gong would provide moments of distraction from routine. If the gong sounded three times, pause and three again, he was wanted at the signal box, probably to carry a message somewhere; if it sounded six times in succession it was fire practice. This meant one shilling extra in the pay packet so it was welcome, but it was far from a daily sound.

The junior porter would not often be granted relief from his duties, routine or otherwise, though some important travellers might receive porterage from the Station Master himself. When Mr. Salmons alighted from the Newport train on his way to London, Station Master Arthur Sabin was there to carry his small attache case! Mr. Salmons held a distinguished position in the area as the head of the established family firm of Salmons of Newport Pagnell, coach bodybuilders. In 1922, under the name of Tickfords Ltd., they were about to produce the firm's own car appropriately called the NP. It was much later that the names of Aston Martin and Lagonda became associated with the firm, and indeed the town.

Sid Sellers was well liked and widely regarded as a railwayman through and through. He first started on the railways in 1918 at the age of 14. He served for 51 years rising to become Signalman, Special Class and retiring in 1968 at the age of 65. He spent his retirement in Bletchley and died in 1982 during the writing of this book.

The Last Journey of the Bedford Times Coach

The passing of the Age of Steam is mourned by thousands, and nostalgia for the early railways has become an industry. Indeed books such as this owe their publication to the widespread interest in the subject, and there are directories filled with the names of societies and organisations dedicated to preserving memories and relics of an age which was elbowed out by new enterprise and innovation. But it was only about 140 years ago that Steam itself was in the process of displacing an earlier age of travel: an age which was not to pass without mourners of its own. *'The period for the annihilation of "four-in-hands" has at length arrived, and the Bedford TIMES Coach has taken its last journey. For 21 years has this favourite drag most chivalrously fought its way; and so uniform and punctual have been its engagements, so complete its appointments, that it had become part and parcel of the "ancient institutions" of this locality. But now manners and customs are changed, and Times too; the natives will no longer go to the Swan-Square to see their old favourite start; the cheerful smack of the whip is usurped by the engine-whistle; and the pleasant journey up the road gives place to a whirl along the rail. Formerly the TIMES was considered an era in travelling, but in these days of rapidity of thought and action, ten miles an hour will not do, nothing short of twenty will satisfy that great family the public; and, as horses cannot do it for the money, steam must . . . And so Bedford has at last made a beginning with steam, and doubtless people will become so fastidious soon, that every town will have its railway, and the turnpike roads will be left for the gipsies and the new police.'*

So wrote the *Bedford Times* newspaper, with a prophetic air, in November 1846 when the Bedford to Bletchley railway was opened to the public. The jubilant crowd at Bedford was celebrating the opening of the first railway in the county, and credit for the achievement was being claimed by civic leaders and businessmen of the ancient town.

Now was the time for nostalgic recollection of a passing era; the colourful coach painted in rich claret and blue with wheels of vivid scarlet; the four horses with shapely heads and powerful legs; the interior richly cushioned in rose coloured silk; the windows with green curtains in winter and scarlet in summer.

For Bedford it would be an unforgettable day, it was a time to celebrate, and for he who wielded the impassioned pen, and fired the feelings of Bedford people, it was a good time for rousing words. He could have a nostalgic feast giving a glossy and cheerful account of the journey of the coach. But there was the hard unassailable fact that despite the luxurious interior, the few who could afford to travel on the *Times* often suffered luxurious hardship *en route*.

The writer on the Bedford Times Newspaper, maybe like the people of Bedford, could not decide whether he wished to celebrate the opening of the new railway more than he wished to lament the passing of the TIMES coach. The Age of Steam was there to stay, and was there to be admired for evermore; but the TIMES had just passed away and deserved a decent funeral. He decided to provide a fitting obituary. — *'No doubt this new state of things will be of great advantage to the community; and, perhaps, we have arrived at that high pitch of enterprise that it was necessary to "lay on the steam", but, nevertheless, we cannot help a sigh for the good old comfortable days when people could afford to take things quietly, and it was an event to travel fifty miles from home by a coach. Neither can we forget the proud displays of "four-in-hand" that have graced the road, such as no other nation could match; nor the delight we have experienced in the trips by the Rockets, Crown Princes, Regulators, Swallows, Ages, Independents, Despatches, Wonders and Times. But this in an AGE when men are taught to be INDEPENDENT of CROWN PRINCES, cease to WONDER at the TIMES kept by REGULATORS, and to DESPATCH themselves by a fiery train that will give a ROCKET the go-by, and think no more of the speed of a SWALLOW, than they would of a CROW! Still we have sometimes yearnings for a few of the customs of the good old TIMES:*

There is an innate feeling clings
Around this mortal clay;
A fondness for familiar things,
That will not wear away.

In our recollection, it was considered a great privilege to get the box seat. Many of the highest rank and attainments have eagerly aspired to a perfection in the art of driving "four-in-hand". It is quite fresh in our recollection, the eclat with which the accomplished Stevenson drove his coach to Brighton, horsed by some of the finest animals in the world, having his livery-servant for a guard, who handed round the silver sandwich-box to prevent the passengers getting down and hindering the professed half-minute change. Nor can Sir Vincent Cotton and his AGE, Lord Edward Thynne, CUM MULTIS ALIIS, be readily forgotten; and the magnificent display of the Mails leaving the Old Post office, who could think of without regret of its discontinuance? And who that ever travelled on the North road, or any other great road of traffic, can forget the brilliancy and usefulness of the stage coaches? Not a town nor village that did not turn out half the population to see its coaches come and go; and we cherish the recollection of the generous feeling that lit up every countenance when there was "a good load". There was a nationality about the stage coach system, and the people seemed proud of their superiority over the travelling appointments of other nations; and well they might. The theoretical Nimrod thought he could not find a better subject for his nimble pen; and he was right in one respect, for his articles on "four-in-hand" received a higher remuneration than many others ten times more sensible and scientific, from ten times sounder writers. But all this brilliancy would not avail the

the system longer; it attained perfection and blazed like a meteor, but has now had an extinguisher put upon it that can never be removed. The go-ahead system has obtained the supremacy— the electric wire has been touched— and all must answer to it— or be left behind. And so, to be consistent, and to keep pace with our neighbours, we must have a rail, and leave the TIMES on the stocks, a memorial of departed greatness; regretting at the same time, that it cannot tell its own tale, and awaken a greater sympathy on its last farewell than we can. It dies with a good name and reputation; and, although many a boy threw a stone at it in its proud progress on the road, we venture to say there are none who would throw a stone at its fair fame now it is gone.'

Like the cortege that had arrived at the graveside, there was little more to do than pay a few last respects, except perhaps to subscribe to a headstone. The writer proudly offered an epitaph.

'No mangled limbs and headless trunks will rise in ghostly horror to haunt its dying hour, and say "Thou didst it" but it will end its time-honoured career amidst the praise and esteem of all who used it, and all who knew it. Amidst all the tears for the departed, there is, nevertheless, one little balm, one cheering circumstance, which will prevent our old friend from entirely sinking into oblivion. If we cannot have a lock of its hair for a keepsake, we shall at least have the pleasure of keeping its likeness: for we find that Mr. Rudge, the artist, has taken its portrait; so that when we grow old we may lift up our crutch, and say to our great-grandchildren, that was the way we travelled by The Bedford TIMES.'

Two readers mourned the passing of the *'time honoured coach'* and displayed their poetic talent in subsequent issues before the year 1846 had passed away. The opening lines of one were

'Oh, monarch of coaches! thy glory is past;
Thou has won thy laurels and run thy last.'

Nearly sixteen years later when the Bletchley to Bedford railway was extended through to Cambridge, the *Bedford Times* newspaper published an account of the occasion. It referred to the Company's new extension as *'the crowning stroke to their railway communication to the four points of the compass'*.

There was no mention of the *'time honoured glory of the four-in-hand'*.

Station Master Gillett's Reward

There were many cases of heavy trains failing to reach the summit of Brogborough Bank. Generally the train would be divided and the front portion taken to Ridgmont, the engine returning later for the rear portion. On occasions a banking engine would assist at the rear.

In 1874 an incident took place where an engine was defeated at Brogborough Bank and the driver's action together with the guard's lack of it, would have ended in disaster if an alert Station Master had not acted quickly.

The Bedford Times waxed indignant in a report of the incident and wanted to see those responsible dealt with severely.

On a dark night, in the October of that year, a coal train comprising 25 wagons and a brake van, was proceeding slowly up the bank bound for Bletchley when it came to a stand still just short of the summit. No doubt the train

Lidlington Station.

69

was over loaded. The driver went to the rear of the engine and uncoupled it from the train. *The Bedford Times* reported that the driver took this action with a view to 'coaxing' the engine. Whatever his reason, it was a disastrous thing to do, without first securing the train. As soon as they were uncoupled the train began to run back; the driver could do no more than sound the engine whistle repeatedly in an attempt to alert the guard, so that he could apply the hand brake in the rear van.

The guard, or brakesman as he was called in those days, apparently did not hear the driver's frantic whistling, and the train careered at increasing speed back down Brogborough Bank. Fortunately however, Station Master Gillett, and his son, at Lidlington did hear the whistle and quickly recognised the urgency of the situation. With little time to spare Station Master Gillett pulled the crossover road points, switching the runaway train from the up line on to the down. The train passed through Ampthill Station at an estimated speed of 45 miles per hour.

Mr. Gillett's quick action averted a terrible and otherwise inevitable crash affecting another goods train standing on the up line at Ampthill Station. The runaway train continued and finally came to a stand still at Cow Bridge, which carries the Midland main line over the Bedford branch line, about seven miles from where the train started its runaway journey!

Meanwhile the engine on the stationary goods train at Ampthill was uncoupled, and with 'officials' accompanying the driver and fireman, they proceeded towards Bedford to take charge of the errant train when it finally came to rest. When they arrived at Cow Bridge, some of the officials went straight to the brake van to see how the brakesman had fared, and found to their astonishment that he was completely unaware of all that had happened. He had no doubt been sound asleep.

The Bedford Times was aware that such incidents were thoroughly investigated, but let it be known in advance what they thought and expected: 'if blame is attached to anyone they ought to be made to remember it and the Company ought to reward Mr. Gillett and his son:

The LNWR did not publicly show their indignation but they did take firm action. Minute No. 7827 of the LNWR Southern Committee of 4th November 1874 stated: 'On the 12th ultimo a special coal train from Sandy came to a stand on the incline between Lidlington and Ridgmont owing to the failure of the engine;

this was detached with the intention of running it forward for assistance, when the whole train, consisting of 25 wagons and a brake van, commenced to run back on the up line in the direction of Bedford. Mr. Gillet the Station Master at Lidlington however, turned the train on to the down line and thus prevented a collision with the 2.30 pm goods train from Cambridge which was standing on the up line at Ampthill Station. The runaway finally stopped at Cowbridge, a distance of about 7 miles from the point at which it started. Bowler, the engine driver of the special train, has been suspended for a fortnight and reduced to the grade of fireman and Dimmock the acting Brakesman has been sent back to Camden Shed and is not to be employed in the capacity of brakesman for six months — a reward of £2 has been paid to Mr. Gillett.'

One can only suppose the *Bedford Times* was satisfied that justice had been done. But what is surprising is that within six years following the incident the crossover points at Lidlington were removed as shown in *Parliamentary Papers LXXXI* page 438 —an *'Alphabetical list of stations used by passenger trains where no points exist.'*

These points had saved a costly crash for £2. It seems the LNWR did not expect such an incident to happen again.

Fifty five years later, a heavy brick train did break loose at the same spot and the rear portion ran back colliding with a train standing in Ampthill Station (renamed Millbrook in 1877). The fireman on the stationary locomotive was crushed to death. After this accident a re-enlightened LMS Railway Company put in trap points up the Brogborough Bank.

Millbrook Station, similar in design to Woburn Sands, Ridgmont, and Fenny Stratford.

On the Cambridge to Bletchley line.

Blow Backs

When one writes about 'blow backs' on steam locomotives, it is like writing about the nasty side of an otherwise nice chap. It is the time when he lashes out for no apparent reason and contrary to his nature. Sometimes these outbursts of temper are laughable but others are unforgivable.

Serious 'blow backs' were not an everyday occurrence. When one did occur, the investigating experts invariably used phrases like 'we cannot be sure'. The use of the blower valve always came under scrutiny and doubts were always expressed as to whether the fireman had used it properly.

It was the *inexplicable* 'blow back' that gave real concern to footplatemen. Tunnels, especially single bore tunnels, provided the classic situation for the serious 'blow back' and so, to lessen the possibility, crews would always open the blower valve before entering. Minor 'blow backs' would occur more often; a flame would suddenly shoot out of the

Sandy Station

firebox like a serpent's tongue and just as quickly return, the fireman receiving perhaps no more than a hot lick. At times such as these the driver was able to laugh at his colleague who would be examining his singed overalls or rubbing a rather warm posterior.

The passing years have allowed us to forgive the steam engine for most of its moments of ill temper, but of the tales that exist about blow backs, inevitably some are serious and some are less so.

On a cold morning a local passenger train was travelling from Bletchley to London. Pieces of tarpaulin were tied to each side of the cab of tank engine No. 2061 to keep out the cold wind since the locomotive was steaming bunker first. There was a sudden explosion in the fire box as Driver Bill Wyeth closed the regulator to coast into Kings Langley Station; the cab was filled with flames that just as quickly returned to the fire box. The train was stopped immediately and Fireman George King jumped out and rolled down a grass bank in an effort to smother his burning clothes. An off duty driver who had been travelling as a passenger assisted in getting the train to Watford, and the guard attended to the badly burned fireman. George was taken to hospital and returned to work some eleven months later with his legs badly scarred.

The engine was taken out of service and it had two days thorough examination at Bletchley Shed. The bunker was emptied of coal in a search for traces of mining explosives. No doubt the blower valve came under very close scrutiny!

Two days later the engine was back in service and placed on a Cambridge passenger train. Driver Johnny Eastaff was told of the engine's recent behaviour and that no fault had been found. Everything was going well, and there was no reason to suspect an imminent 'blow back'. But as the train was approaching Sandy with the blower valve well on there was, once again, an explosion in the fire box. Flames shot out into the cab. They quickly returned from whence they came leaving the fireman minus most of his jacket. The unfortunate fellow spent a day in Cambridge Hospital, then soon afterwards decided that railways were not his vocation and he departed the service.

Further examination did not result in a decisive answer to the problem; it was thought by some people that 'bunker first running' created conditions for back draft down the chimney. This was no answer for most of us; Bletchley men did many miles bunker first on tank engines without 'blow backs', serious or minor.

It was during the following year, 1955, that the 'Dunstable Dasher', the little push and pull, or steam motor train, running between Leighton Buzzard and Luton Bute Street, misbehaved resulting in loss of life.

On 20th April, engine No. 1222, a 2–6–2 LMS tank, left Luton at 8.30am when about three quarters of a mile from Dunstable Town Station, a fierce 'blow back' literally blew Driver Burchett and Fireman Capp from the footplate. The two-coach train continued on its journey, running past two stations and a busy crossing for two miles until the guard stopped the runaway train by using the brake in his van. Driver Burchett was taken to hospital; people living near the line saw him fall from the engine. He was suffering from severe shock and burns, and it was sometime before he could be interviewed by the Ministry of Transport Inspector. Unfortunately Fireman Capp died of his injuries.

Again the engine was examined thoroughly by experts at Bletchley Shed. Coal was emptied from the bunker and sifted for traces of explosives; other apparatus that could have played a part in the accident also came under close scrutiny. Visual examination of the cab showed badly scorched paintwork, and so intense was the heat in those brief moments, the spare headlamp in the cab had completely disintegrated.

Colonel McMullen, Ministry of Transport Inspector, in his report of the accident, could find no defect on the engine or anything to suggest that a mining explosive had found its way into the coal. In his view the accident most probably occurred because the blower valve had not been opened before the regulator was closed.

Driver Burchett said at the MOT enquiry that prior to closing the regulator at the summit of the bank, just before running into Dunstable Town Station, he told his fireman to open the blower valve, and he confirmed he had done so.

Colonel McMullen, in his concluding remarks, admitted that the real cause of 'blow backs' was not

The Dunstable Dasher

known but it was known that they were more likely to occur if, when running, the blower valve was not opened before the regulator was closed, and that more frequently they take place in tunnels. He also thought that rows of high trees along the line could help set up the condition.

In this particular case it seemed to the Colonel that a protracted explosion of unburnt gases in the firebox could have taken place. He discussed the matter with BTC officers who agreed to examine the question of 'blow backs' to see whether conditions under which they occurred could be determined more exactly, and whether more positive and practical methods of preventing them could be found. The report ended: *'Modern facilities enable such an investigation to be undertaken and so far as is known this will be the first of its kind. This may be regarded as satisfactory'.*

This did not help the poor fireman, and as it was nearing the end of the steam age, it is doubtful if the report helped anyone.

With little more than ten years to run before the steam engine would disappear from British Railways, it was rather late in the day to have a 'first' investigation, even if modern facilities did enable it. It was, perhaps, like a Royal Commission; an ideal way of shelving a problem.

An anecdote I will entitle 'Hollis Wheeler's unlucky day' is far more typical of a 'blow back' and can be recalled with a smile.

Driver Hollis Wheeler's unlucky day probably would have begun when he was awoken by the Call Boy at about 3 am; I was his fireman and my memory of it began when we left the Loco Shed at 4.30 with an LNWR freight engine, (an old Super D), to pick-up a train at Swanbourne for Bicester Ordnance Sidings.

The engine was brought to a stand behind another in the Oxford Bay, just beside the dark and silent refreshment rooms. During a short wait in the early hours most drivers would sit upon the half-moon wooden seat, and many would be inclined to put their feet on the drip plate above the fire hole door and rest back against the slender handrail. Despite the precarious position it was bliss to close ones eyes for a couple of minutes at that unearthly hour. But in those two minutes on Hollis's unlucky morning, another engine came up behind and misjudged the distance in the dark. A rather heavy Hollis was shaken abruptly from his snooze when he landed heavily on the floor of the cab. The poor chap almost crawled on to the platform, holding his back, and sat there on a laundry basket moaning and cursing his misfortune. Some ten minutes later Hollis returned to his engine and, still holding his back, we continued our journey.

On reaching Bicester we discovered that the Ordnance Sidings were not yet open. Waiting for the signal to enter, the Driver still a little subdued but no longer complaining of his back, began the ritual of making tea. It was a pleasant red fire well banked up under the door, so out came the shovel and on to the blade went the enamel tea can filled with water. The shovel was gently placed into the firebox. Hollis squatted down, pensively looking into the fire, holding the shovel handle.

Just then the Oxford 'up' passenger train passed by; out shot the serpent's tongue with a bang and Hollis was lying on the coal in the tender with legs outstretched. His look told of the words to follow. Amidst some unholy language he rose to his feet, with a very red face.

I turned away, trying hard to suppress a laugh. There was no real damage done and, if the boot had been on the other foot, Hollis with a look of amusement would probably have asked, 'Was it hot mate?'.

Brewing up.

The Local Goods Train

The local goods trains had a character of their own, and during years of both war and peace they never ceased to run. Until the lines no longer carried traffic and the steam era was almost past, they served the country stations with sometimes only a single wagon load, and even smaller consignments which were conveyed in a Tariff van. During the last 40 years of their existence 'the goods' altered very little. Before World War II they started their journey from Bletchley Yard, and later when Swanbourne Sidings were built some started from there, otherwise a local goods train in the 1940s would be no different from one in the 1920s.

A total of 97 miles of branch line was associated with the Oxford to Cambridge and so, with sidings at nearly every station plus a few others way out in the country, there had to be more than one local goods train. There were the Bedford local goods, the Gamlingay, the two Banburys, the Brackley, and the two locals worked one from Cambridge and the other from Oxford. The Oxford local had once been given the number '19', and it continued to have that title unofficially until the last steam engine had gone. The Gamlingay spent so much time shunting vegetables and other miscellaneous traffic on the way out, that the crew were relieved for the return trip.

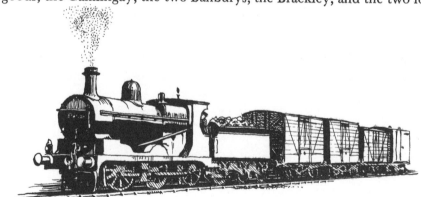

A Lanky or Gracie Fields.

79

The Banbury was traversed daily by two local goods, one going through to Banbury and the other terminating at Brackley. Either train could have been hauled by an ex L&YR 0—6—0 engine known as a *Lanky* or *Gracie Fields*. Their lifting type injectors and the constant overheating of injector delivery pipes did not endear them to Bletchley enginemen. Another likely engine could have been a LNWR *Cauliflower*, an 0—6—0 with, quite possibly, wooden brake blocks on the tender. Both engines shared the same design of narrow cab roof; wind and wet weather across the Banbury Line were never welcome. However, later on the *Midland Freight Four* did occasionally come on the scene. If removal of discomfort was luxury, then this was luxury. The engine for the Banbury local came off the Loco at 5.45am possibly coupled to the Sandy coal engine, and after picking up the guards on No. 1 platform, it went to Swanbourne Sidings to link up with their respective trains. The Banbury goods soon departed, due to shunt out and deliver wagons to Buckingham and Brackley.

It was later in the morning when the Brackley goods engine came off the Loco Shed to leave Swanbourne Sidings at about 9.30 to deliver and pick up at all stations and sidings to Brackley, except Verney Junction, which received its local deliveries from the various freight trains taking traffic for the Metropolitan line.

Let us follow the events and fortunes that might befall an engine crew during a typical day on the Brackley Goods. Its first call, after departure from Swanbourne Sidings, was Swanbourne Station where signalman Fred Walters would be waiting on the platform complete in immaculate bow-tie. After having locked the booking office securely, he would greet the guard with a 'Hello Bill, two empties to pick up'. Guard Billy Norman would exchange greetings with him and impart the information that there were three loads of coal to detach. The tariff van was opened and the small consignments unloaded on to the platform. Then with the use of the annett key, the points were opened and closed by the signalman whilst Bill shunted the siding.

Upon departure for Winslow an onlooker may have noticed a two finger sign from the guard to a plate-layer. It was not a victory sign or a rude gesture; it was an order for two rabbits on his return.

At Winslow, the tariff van would be backed into the goods shed for sorting. Shunting out empty wagons, and placing loads, took care of the next 40 minutes or so. It is worth noting that shunt movements meant the driver had to reverse his engine, which, if it was a LNWR *Cauliflower,* meant 18 turns of the reversing wheel which was nearly waist height and needed considerable effort to turn. There was much heaving and sweating in the warmer weather. It was therefore understandable that shunt movements were saved by knocking wagons into the sidings. It was equally understandable when, after an hour's shunting, an exasperated driver would lean over the side of his cab and say rather impatiently to the guard 'Are you getting these bloody wagons in number order?'

The sidings with large goods sheds such as Winslow and Buckingham had their checkers who were responsible for the shed and looking after the local traders by ensuring the wagons were placed near their carts or lorries. They knew their yard and their traders well. They helped the guard in the shunting operation and all were rural characters who often had a side line in the selling of vegetables and eggs or both.

After shunting was completed and wagons placed, the engine would be taken to the water column to fill the tender. By this time the down train was probably due and the train would be shunted across the road for it to pass.

Padbury was next stop. The 'single line staff' had been taken from signalman Charlie Batsford at Verney Junction. He stood on the adjoining line with the staff held just above his head for it to be grasped by the fireman as the train passed slowly by. A few small consignments in the tariff van were unloaded on to the platform for Mrs Allen as she, in turn, informed the guard that two empty wagons required picking up; there would be a few minutes shunting, a coal truck would be slipped, and the empty wagons were on the train, bound for Buckingham.

Padbury Station.

There would be an exchange of staff again at Buckingham Station and, if there was not work to be done there the engine would go down to the goods yard where the staff unlocked the points into the siding. It was unlikely that the brief stand in the station would not pass without some conversation between the enginemen and signalman Harold Plant. Complimentary remarks about the station gardens would have been received with a smile from Harold; however any reference to the competition at Verney Junction would be met by a grunt!

On arrival at the yard Billy Norman would come into his own; all his skill and confidence, a characteristic of that generation of goods guards, would immediately become evident. Bill, hefty and middle aged would alight, and taking the shunting pole from the floor of his van, he would place it over his shoulder and walk off without haste. He would greet the checker, who would reply with some remark about the weather; then there would be an exchange of information of what was on the train, what was to be detached, placed and picked up. Bill would then walk down the train and place his pole between two wagons at the appropriate place. The pole would first be laid across the buffer then with a slight heave and a twist the heavy coupling fell with a bang. This was followed immediately by a hand signal to the driver and the shunting was in progress. Without apparent hurry or effort the whole operation was accomplished with astonishing speed: Bill's shunting plan had been formulated in his mind the moment he was told the requirements —there

Staff, token or tablet: made of leather with a white handle.

A shunting pole: the wooden handles were usually made of hickory.

was never a conference of 'ways and means' . . . the wagons just moved from one road to the other. Finally the engine and tariff van went to the goods shed where the small consignments were dealt with. The engine would then be taken back onto the single line and with its train ready marshalled for quick and easy shunting it would be on its way to Brackley.

There is little doubt that Billy had exchanged opinions with the checker on which horse was going to win the 2.30 at Newmarket.

In passing ganger Jack Rawlings' cottage at Radclive Farm crossing, a few lumps of coal would slide off the footplate at the front gate, and Mrs Rawlings would acknowledge the accident with a hurried wave at the window.

Bacon House public siding would seldom have any traffic, but Bill would remember the times when wagons, in and out, were a regular feature of the day's work, and a glass of wine from the lady at the crossing house might be just as regular. No doubt she had appreciated a few lumps of coal, too. — There were a lot of rabbits along the line and several drivers and firemen would purchase them cheaply perhaps for the office workers back at Bletchley who never saw the line. But there were some who kept an eagle eye open for a platelayer's snare and if one was seen, they might stop and pocket the rabbit. The plate-layers knew this happened and on one occasion Jack Rawlings tied a note on one of his snares 'Keep your bloody thieving hands off, the rabbit is ours' The rabbit still disappeared and Jack found the brief but cheeky reply 'Thanks we had it'.

As the train approached Brackley, Signalman Arthur Marriott would be waiting to take the staff and ask Billy Norman what shunting was required in the Brackley yard. Here it was necessary for the engine to run round the train, their loads having been disgorged in the goods shed for collection by the various traders.

The Rabbit Catcher

83

Arthur would have the kettle on the stove in his box so that when shunting was over the train crew could adjourn there for tea. Billy Norman would be seen to pass a small piece of folded white paper to the signalman. Its thickness made it obvious that a coin of some description was inside. It was accepted quietly and without surprise. The secretive transaction concerned Billy's bet; which horse the money was to be placed on would more than likely be discussed later when all had settled down to tea.

Arthur was the bookies runner and in his own pleasant manner he collected bets from railwaymen and other punters. He was in telephone communication with Jimmy Trotman at the next box at Cockley Brake, who was also engaged in bookmaking. Although the box at Cockley Brake was the most isolated on the line it was the junction with the SMJ (Stratford and Midland Junction Railway) from Blisworth, which put him in contact with those on another cross country line.

If tea in Brackley signalbox commenced with speculation about the winner of the 2.30 it would quite likely turn later to Rules and Regulations, a popular subject in those days, and invariably this lead to disagreement; so out would come the General or Sectional Appendix and the Rule Book to settle the point. Billy had a dry sense of humour, and doggerel of his own which was appreciated by many railwaymen. He spoke with a broad rural dialect, and he was very much a countryman, but he certainly knew the rules and regulations. He could not recite them like a parrot but had learned them by experience, and in mess room arguments he was seldom wrong.

While shunting was in operation at Brackley, the Banbury local goods was returning home. On arrival the engine would carry out some shunting in the yard although much of this would have been done by the engine off the 8.0 am passenger from Bletchley before it returned with the afternoon passenger train. If it was Thursday, cattle market day, the noise of the cattle in the dock pens or cattle trucks would often be louder than the shunting. A *Midland Freight Four* engine off the SMJ which had completed its shunting would be waiting for a train load of cattle for Northampton.

After the local goods had completed its shunting at Banbury it would be put on the table to turn: then the tender was filled with water. While the fireman threw out a few pieces of red hot clinker from the fire, the driver put a few drops of oil in the slide bar cups on the links. Then there would be a wash up in the shovel. When that was finished the shovel would be placed in the mouth of the firebox with a tea can, filled with spring water from the column. When it boiled, tea was served. The same shovel having attained a red hot heat, would be declared clean and would quite likely be used to fry egg, bacon and the occasional sausage.

The *Cauliflower* afforded very little dining comfort. The half moon seats on either side of the cab would be utilised as tables for the egg and bacon. Standing with knife and fork was no hardship under the circumstances. It was generally thought that the locomotive scored over the L&Y engine which had no seats. The tea can and two cups on the drip plate above the fire hole door was convenient and ensured the tea kept its heat. The train staff would be handed over by the signalman as he leaned out of the box. There would be an exchange of hand signals between fireman and guard, and they were on their way. A regulation whistle for the farm crossing shortly after departure would usually gain a wave from the lady at the farmhouse or someone working in the fields.

Passing Farthinghoe's tiny wooden station nestling peacefully in the cutting, the crew might be excused for believing that all life there was extinct. On rare occasions they might just notice the door ajar and old Jim the porter briefly peering through. The fox that had casually watched the train's early morning descent into Banbury from the safety of the upland slope near Cockley Brake was now no longer to be seen.

Enamel tea can.

A change of train staff, taken on the move, at Cockley Brake did not allow lengthy conversation. The same procedure at Brackley would be accompanied by a whistle to the train crew having a final mug of tea in the signalbox and they, in turn, would hold up the tea can and a mug. — The usual greeting on such occasions.

When the down passenger train to Banbury passed it was time for the

Farthinghoe
Station

Brackley goods to make for home. As the train crew descended the signalbox steps, the argument about rules and regulations could still be in full swing. At the last minute one or other of the crew would remember to pick up a bundle of cabbage plants which Arthur had grown on his allotment behind the signalbox and which he had wrapped in a weekly notice.

The train comprised mainly empty wagons on the return journey. The empties placed on the front road in Buckingham yard were now ready to be picked up. It could be that the up passenger was hard on their heels at Winslow and the signalman would keep his starting signal on. He would stand at the open window, his arms crossed high in the air to denote they were to back into the refuge siding or across to the down line to let the passenger go by.

It was, by necessity, a slow journey approaching Swanbourne Station. If Ernie Dickens was not still working on the length, Billy Norman's two rabbits would be suitably hung on a stick firmly stuck into the ground to enable him to reach out and catch them as he passed.

Swanbourne sidings were the end of the journey and the train was left securely in the reception sidings ready for the shunt engine to begin its work. Unless a trip train was required at Bletchley, the engine would go right away to Bletchley Loco yard with all the train crew on the footplate. Billy Norman would probably put the finishing touches to his time sheet on the way in before alighting on to the platform at Bletchley Station. The Cauliflower would come to rest on the ashpit to await disposal and servicing. The driver would have only one more duty . . . to make out a repair card and to sign off.

By the post war years all the *Cauliflowers* were 50 years old or more; some repair or other would always be necessary, so there would always be something for the driver to write upon the repair card. 'Piston-packing blowing through', 'engine not steaming', and 'tender brakes adjusting', were so frequently required they were entered on the card as regularly as the date.

A Cauliflower.

A stroke post.

The Legend of Denbigh Hall

For railwaymen, *Denbigh Hall Bridge* has always been a landmark. With such a distinguished name one could be forgiven for imagining that the bridge was sited close by a ducal hunting lodge or the turreted home of a wealthy merchant. But the truth is that *Denbigh Hall* was nothing more illustrious than a pub, and often a rather rowdy one at that. The pub had been there for centuries but became nationally known because of the bridge which carried the railway over Watling Street; ironically, the bridge was the cause of the pub's ultimate decline and disappearance.

In the 17th century and 18th century the area had a reputation for murder and brutality. In 1617 it is recorded 'a stranger slayne, found in Wyrchley Wood.' The inn lay at the foot of Rickley Wood Hill. In 1654 a man named Bunch who committed murder on the spot was hanged there, for at that time gallows were quite common ornaments along Watling Street, and the foot of Rickley Hill was a regular site for hanging until 1699 when they were removed for good. The character of the place did not improve, for in 1741 a child and the owner of a refreshment booth situated at the

Denbigh Hall Inn at the junction of the main line, and Watling Street.

site, were murdered there, and in 1766 the Rector of Tingewick was attacked by a highwayman just north of the inn. The Rector shot him dead. A year later Richard Braund of Shenley was found dead close by; he had been shot in the head. It was locally presumed that he had been attempting to rob a coach passenger. Neither did matters improve in the next century for in 1805 a local shoemaker was robbed and murdered there.

One story goes, the inn was originally called the *Marquis of Granby*, or *Granby Head*, and was inhabited by an old woman named Moll Norris. One winter's night the Earl of Denbigh's carriage was stopped by snow-drifts and he had to take shelter at the inn. When about to leave he called for his bill. The old woman, un-familiar with the term 'bill', brought him a hatchet. The Earl's family confirmed, much later, that one of their ancestors had once stopped there and was made so comfortable, he used it often as a halfway house to London. Moll died in 1698, but it is thought that descendants of the old Earl continued calling there and on one occasion were accompanied by Lady Denbigh who had her portrait drawn in pastels by a 13-year old boy who was staying at the inn. The boy subsequently became Sir Thomas Lawrence and the portrait became part of the family collection.

The inn was not so well regarded by others. A local diarist once wrote that a nearby cottage was pulled down in 1706 but. 'Denbigh Hall, alas, still stands'. Also, a later historian wrote that the inn, 'had been acquired by Mr. Calcraft the Brewer who, like many other brewers, was buying up inns to prevent, no doubt, other brewers from supplying their bad beer, and having the privilege himself '

The new railway line from London reached *Denbigh Hall* early in 1838. A temporary station was erected there, and for five months until the bridge was built, and the vast engineering work at Kilsby Tunnel completed, passengers for Birmingham and elsewhere were met by stage coach. Those five months were the busiest in the life of *Denbigh Hall.*

While the engineering work continued, there was an unending flow of stage coaches arriving and depart-ing with passengers wishing to make use of the incomplete line. The resourceful landlord, Thomas Holdom, did a roaring trade. He turned the private quarters of the inn into additional bars and dining rooms; parlours were converted into dormitory areas at night. His pigsties were turned into additional stabling.

For a short while *Denbigh Hall* became a thriving, bustling road house, offering as much accommodation

as possible for both man and beast, but at the very lowest standards. It was soon surrounded by gypsies, hucksters, and all the rogues of the region. It was said the landlord made so much money in that short time he kept it in milk churns in his bedroom.

As each train arrived from London it was met by a string of coaches for provincial towns. Travellers for Birmingham could leave London at 7.30 am, catching a stage coach from *Denbigh Hall* at 10 o'clock and continuing to Rugby to leave by train from there at 2.30 in the afternoon. The drive between *Denbigh Hall* and Rugby took 4¼ hours through hilly and beautiful country.

There were never enough coaches or horses to meet the demand, and at the time of the Coronation of Queen Victoria there was almost a riot for transport at Rugby to link up with the London train. The price of seats took an astronomical rise.

The bridge gradually neared its completion. Built on the site of an old Roman ford the railway had to straddle the turnpike road at an angle of 25 degrees. The engineers decided against a skew bridge which would have needed a span of 80 feet; they chose instead to build a simple bridge, square to the road with only a 34 feet span, but with a total length of 200 feet. Travellers on the turnpike had the impression of riding through a tunnel.

The roaring trade and the quick rise in the fortunes of

Denbigh Hall Bridge: until
1838, the end of the line.

the landlord of the inn were soon to end. On 17th September 1838 the line was opened for the first London to Birmingham railway service. Wolverton became the main intermediate stopping place: all trains stopped there, the locomotives changed, and passengers could obtain refreshment.

The inn went back to its original status and gradually declined. It saw some pleasant days between the wars when on summer Sunday evenings families would stroll across the fields from Bletchley to the old *Denbigh Inn* where children could have lemonade and arrowroot biscuit. When a Brewster Session objected to the lack of running water on the premises the brewery company closed it down, and it was demolished in 1957.

For over a century signal boxes in the vicinity of the bridge have been known by the name of *Denbigh Hall*. Now the junction has taken on the job of keeping the name alive; a bold sign announces that travellers are passing *Denbigh Hall Junction*.

The wrong Wrong Line Order

Driver 'Gudgeon' Felce was anxiously holding the regulator handle of an old 'D', an engine then well past its prime. It was a dark wet night and behind, were 60 wagon loads of bricks. Gudgeon was cursing the weather, and speculating as to whether or not they would succeed in hauling the heavy load up the incline and over the brow to Ridgmont. He was constantly looking for the gradient sign which marked the summit. Young Tom Read, his fireman, was raw and inexperienced, but he felt some consolation in the fact that the lad was keeping a full head of steam.

Suddenly there came a roar from the chimney and sparks flew into the sky. This was followed by a quick easing of the regulator and a frantic pulling back and forth of the sand valve handle. A decrease in the roar gave hope but, on repeating this procedure there was an even greater roar, sparks rks flew everywhere and there was a spinning of wheels. The driver continued to open and close the regulator, whilst Tom shook the sand valves with equal fervour; this led eventually to comparative silence as the engine came to a halt, exhausted. There was no hope of setting back the wagons on the brake van to ease the couplings and make a sudden opening of the regulator for a final effort, because the train was on the trap points.

Gradient post at the Brogborough Bank summit

Cursing mildly, the driver told Tom to run back, on the offside, to see the guard, get a Wrong Line Order and to tell him to halve the train so that it could be taken to Ridgmont, in two portions before recoupling ready for London.

Past the 60 wagons, in the rain and darkness went Tom, running as fast as he could but hindered by the weather and the uneven ballast on

93

the track. The driver's instructions were well imprinted in his mind, but he had little real knowledge of Wrong Line Orders. Pat Duffy was anxiously waiting in his brake van when Tom arrived to repeat the driver's instructions. Pat was also inexperienced, but he had a better idea of the drill.

Out of his bag came the Wrong Line Orders; was it an 'A' form colour pink, or a 'C' form colour white? Pat decided it must be a white form and quickly penned in the required information. Away ran Tom back along the uneven track, whilst Pat started to pin down individual wagon brakes on the rear portion of the train.

When Tom reached the engine and produced the white form, Gudgeon let out a roar which finished with an utterance about Pat's lack of intelligence and doubtful parentage. It was a *pink* form that was required, so Tom set off again back along the track past the now familiar 60 wagon loads of bricks. The guard had by now pinned down several wagon brakes and uncoupled half the train. A new pink form was found and signed accordingly with the aid of Pat's paraffin handlamp. Away went Tom once again. Arriving exhausted by his marathon,

Ridgmont Station showing the Bedford Arms Public house.

he felt in his pocket for the order. Again driver Gudgeon let out a blasphemous roar and this time it was *Tom's* parentage that came into doubt. Tom stood there on the footplate wet and bedraggled, having to admit he had lost his pink Wrong Line Order. 'Go back and find it or get a fresh one', said Gudgeon, with several more unkind remarks. Back once more went Tom along the familiar route but about two wagons from the brake van, and visible even in the darkness, was the pink Wrong Line Order sticking to the end of a sleeper. Tom returned along the 58 wagons for the last time.

Away to Ridgmont, with the first portion of the train, went the now speechless and unappreciative Gudgeon. The wagons were backed into the sidings and the wet and soggy Wrong Line Order was somehow countersigned by the signalman before the crew returned for the other portion of the train. The rear portion was then brought to Ridgmont and left on the main line whilst the front portion was picked up again and recoupled.

In the confusion the wet and dejected guard had completely forgotten the cardinal rule: to protect the rear of his train with detonators. All's well that ends well, the raw inexperienced guard and fireman were considerably wiser, and even Gudgeon cooled down later to become his more jovial self.

Detonators dated 1887: modern detonators are made by the same firm.

95

Paraffin hand lamp.

Tool Nippers and Clangers

It was often said that the original platelayers were the farm workers who, when railways first came, jumped over the fence to earn a shilling a week more.

Platelayers moved in gangs, often having to stay away from home; their successors, the permanent way men, traditionally lived close by the line and had allotted lengths of track to maintain. Apart from the up-keep of the track itself, they were responsible for drainage, grass cutting, fencing and inevitably, as countrymen, they would become involved in side-lines such as the catching of rabbits.

In the 1920s most platelayers had started their railway careers in

the previous century. The local 'ganger' with his team of platelayers would tend a 'length' of track, with a cabin, usually built of sleepers, as a shelter and a place for a midday meal. At Bletchley there would be a large gang of 'relayers', who might operate anywhere from London to Coventry, and also on the branch lines. Whenever they worked outside the immediate area of Bletchley they would have to lodge, for which they would each receive an allowance of 1/– or 1/6 per night, but which might be lost if the time-keeper heard that the platelayer had cycled home for the night. Generally the platelayers would be away from home for a week at a time, and usually during that spell a lot of beer would be consumed. Some platelayers were renowned for their drinking capacity; one old ganger, named Thecker Dickens, perferring strong beer, was known to add the contents of a bottle of *Daddies Sauce* to give his ale some bite.

As the gang moved on, it would be the job of the 'tool nipper' to precede them with a wagon-load of tools for the men to start work on the Monday morning. It was also the job of the tool nipper to find their lodgings. On arrival at a place of work he would call at various houses in the area; often they were houses of local railwaymen, or sometimes places that had had previously taken lodgers. Over the years some of the lodgings became well known.

A small thatched cottage on the outskirts of Winslow was often used as a billet for platelayers. How many men it could accommodate at one time can only be guessed: it could not have been many, because the tiny cottage was already crammed full of dogs. The establishment was run by an eccentric old lady named Jenny Rush who was well known to many platelayers over the years. In the late 1920s, Jenny Rush was getting old. A little lad by the name of Reg Waters, (who was later to become a permanent way man) would sometimes carry a hot midday meal from his granny's house to Jenny's cottage. One such day in 1927 Reg could get no answer when he knocked at the door and some men, working close by, suggested that Reg should find the local policeman. When the policeman arrived he could get no answer either,

The arm band of the permanent way men's lookout.

Fogmen's oil lamp with yellow top and handle.

despite some very hard knocking. He suggested that Reg should climb through one of the small windows and open the door from the inside. The moment he was in, he was set upon by a crowd of hungry yapping dogs. Someone quickly passed the dinner through the window, and Reg promptly spilt it on the floor. The famished dogs left Reg alone, which enabled him to dislodge the poker which had been securing the front door. They found Jenny half conscious on the floor of her bedroom. Poor Jenny recovered but was later taken to the local workhouse where she eventually died.

Platelayers were experts at catching rabbits and pheasants too, if they came their way. Their skills were passed on to the permanent way men, who have always had regular customers amongst the train crews. Rabbits 'drains', originally laid on the railway banks at the turn of the century, are still in use. A 'Y' shaped drain from the line cess is laid down the bank with two ends of the drain left open and one made into a 'no through road'. When the rabbit runs for cover it will hide in the blanked off end, then to fulfil an order from a driver or a fireman the two open ends of the drain are sealed off. When required for delivery one end is opened up and, with a piece of briar for encouragement, the rabbit is bagged.

At one time fogging duty was an important part of a permanent way man's life. When fog came down in the daytime the men on duty would know where they were required, and proceed from the signal box with a fogman's lamp to position themselves at a distant signal where they usually had a small sentry-box equipped with detonators for the line. A fire was started in a 'fire-devil' and the coloured light from the hand lamp would be displayed in a prominent position. When fog came down at night the signalman would send out a call boy who would alert a permanent way man, and he in turn would alert others who were scheduled for fogging duty. Some outlying villages had fogmen's cottages where the signalman was able to sound a bell. Fogging duties disappeared with automatic colour-light signalling.

Permanent way men ate their midday meal in the relative comfort of their cabins, but the earlier platelayers would sit on the grass, or under a bridge, for their meal and, with a

Lookout's whistle

Permanent way men's hut with a platform gauge
hanging on the outside wall. To the right is a
ladder rack.

clasp knife, take a slice of a 'Bucks clanger'. In the Winslow area it would be referred to as a 'Ten to One', which could refer to the time of the day it was eaten, but it was generally assumed in Winslow that a clanger contained ten pieces of potato to one of meat. The clanger was the staple diet. With potato, onion, meat or bacon at one end, and jam or apple at the other, the whole lot was held together in an envelope made of flour and suet. Tied up in a pudding cloth, with the middle tied extra tight to keep the ingredients separate, it was boiled for a long time. Permanent way men would reheat them on their stove, but for the old platelayers hygiene was not heard of. They would balance them on one side of a flaming fire-devil or on an improvised brick fire.

By the time it was eaten, the clanger might be as black and crunchy as a piece of coke. On Mondays, the platelayers would carry wicker baskets filled with clangers when they were to lodge away for a week. On Wednesdays their wives would each deliver another basketful to be sent, free of charge, to the nearest station to where the gang was working. A four-wheeled barrow loaded with wicker baskets was a common sight on Wednesdays.

It must not be assumed that all wives were adept at making the Bucks clanger. There were platelayers who would indulge in bantering rivalry as to whose clanger contained most meat, and there are stories, maybe apocryphal, of the exceptional qualities of the clanger.

Fogman's hut.

There is a story of a crow that died choking on a piece of clanger it found discarded in the grass: and another about George Windsor of Stoke Hammond who threw his halfeaten clanger and managed to stun a passing rat. Whatever the qualities of the Bucks clanger the gang of platelayers returned home at the end of the week, each carrying two empty wicker baskets.

A Bucks clanger.

The Bigots of Buckingham

Buckingham Station opened in 1850 and, for the first fifty years of its existence, witnessed more pomp and ceremonial decoration than most country stations.

Buckingham itself held the status of Borough, but having the Duke of Buckingham's palatial grounds on its doorstep at Stowe, it is not surprising the town became accustomed to frequent celebrations, and much high ceremony. The civic dignitaries became used to toadying to higher mortals such as dukes, marquises and royal dignitaries

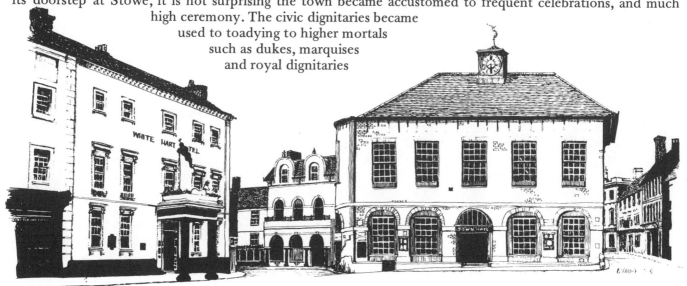

so that it is not surprising that when the radical trumpet playing Salvationists attempted to preach and make music, Buckingham found it very hard to accept. Hitherto, such noise in the sleepy Borough had been reserved for aristocratic occasions and a request by the Salvationists to hire the Town Hall was considered an audacity city.

The Marquis of Chandos (later the Duke of Buckingham) would use the station frequently. Not only had he great political power, but he was Chairman of the London and North Western Railway (from 1853 to 1861); it was then the largest joint stock company in the world.

In 1861 the Marquis resigned his chairmanship of the LNWR because of pressure from the railway directors in the north of England, and in the same year, upon the death of his father, he succeeded to the Dukedom.

The fortunes of Stowe were already in decline when the railway came to Buckingham so the Duke, by necessity, became a 'working duke'. J.K. Fowler in *Echoes of Old County Life* stated that as Marquis of Chandos he resided at Wootton; he often supervised the labourers on that estate who were looking after land drainage and were cutting water courses.

As Chairman of the London and North Western Railway, he often drove the engine from London for long distances, carefully logging every hundredweight of coal consumed and meticulously noting the use of oil and cotton waste.

He became Governor of Madras in 1875 and on his return in 1881 the station was gaily decked with flags and evergreens; the Mayor, as would be expected, was there to greet him. A procession departed from the station, no doubt in order of importance, and including the local MP, magistrates, councillors and aldermen, the coroner, recorder, vicar, tenantry and local townspeople. There was a similar to-do four years later when he was welcomed home with his second bride.

After all this, the arrival of the Salvation Army in about 1887 seemed to have no dignity at all. The Borough's local government and many other citizens did not want the new Salvation Army in their town, and when the Salvationists made an application for the use of the Town Hall a number of ratepayers formed themselves into a committee and obtained a meeting with the mayor in his chambers. Whatever transpired in the council chamber led to the application being refused, as were subsequent requests, although the hall was let for other functions.

One such application was submitted when Commandant Herbert Booth, Major Oliphant and the 'Iron Horse Artillery of the Salvation Army' wished to visit Buckingham. It was met with a measure of sympathy from Councillor Holton who offered them the use of a large building in the old tanyard in Hunter Street.

It is generally accepted that the police and many leading citizens, as well as the rowdy element in the borough, had been watching for an opportunity to bring the Salvation Army within the meshes of a new bye-law. They placed two Salvationists before the bench, charging them with the unlawful playing of musical instruments in the town. The victims chose 14 days in Aylesbury Gaol rather than paying the £2 fine.

However, the Salvationists were not without a champion. It came in the form of the *Bucks Flying Post*, a newspaper owned by Sir Harry Verney of Claydon House and Herbert Leon of Bletchley Park.

The *Bucks Flying Post* called the citizens of Buckingham 'The Bigots of Buckingham' adding that the magistrates were notoriously opposed to the Salvation Army. In fact, the newspaper went so far as to accuse some councillors of enacting the new law simply to penalise Salvationists.

Salvation Army supporters flocked to Buckingham Station to witness Captain Deans' and Lieutenant Morris' departure for gaol but the Borough Police, expecting a demonstration, smuggled the two prisoners into a horse and trap and took them to Padbury Station.

Salvationists of the late 19

The North Front of Stowe.

It must have been an unhappy day for the Bigots of Buckingham when, after serving their sentences, the two Salvationists returned to a tumultuous welcome. Excursion trains brought Salvation Army members from Northampton, Oxford, Bletchley, Wolverton, Bicester, Castlethorpe and Roade. Defiantly the 25 strong Northampton Salvation Army Band marched through the town.

On 26th March, 1889 the duke died. On 2nd April a special funeral train complete with mourners left Buckingham Station for Quainton Road and the Brill Tramway, that little line which would take him to his final resting place, in the family tomb at Wootton.

There was no male heir and the title became extinct. Stowe passed to the late duke's eldest daughter, Lady Mary, who had the title Baroness Kinloss.

Buckingham Station was the scene of various ceremonies until the end of the century and no doubt the burgesses of Buckingham continued to take part; in order of precedence. Stowe was leased to the Comte-de-Paris, but only briefly. While he was there HRH Princess of Wales visited him incognito. The Comte died at Stowe in 1894, and HRH Prince of Wales with many other distinguished mourners came by train to Buckingham. It was again a special train that conveyed the body to Weybridge for interment. In 1898 the Prince of Wales came to Stowe again. This time the station was decorated with red, green and white bunting and plumes of feathers. The Prince was on his way to review the *Royal Bucks Hussars* who were on manoeuvres at Stowe.

The next century saw some very different scenes at Buckingham Station. In 1921 the Stowe estate came up to auction and in that 19-day sale the remaining glories of palatial Stowe were scattered across the world. Alexander Pope once described Stowe, *As near an approach to Elysium as English soil and climate will permit, for what art and opulence can command is here collected'*. In 19 days it was gone for ever.

The new residents at Stowe did not bring ceremony to railway travel at Buckingham; boys are seldom respecters of dignity, whether they are public school boys or not.

Regular vacation specials ran for Stowe School, between Buckingham and Euston, and these continued until 1965 after, incidentally, the line was closed to ordinary passenger traffic. On these 'specials' merriment and high spirits were such that ticket collection at either end was almost impossible. It was generally a ten coach train, and Buckingham Station platform was only four coaches long. As the train drew into Buckingham so doors flew open and boys jumped down onto the ballast, over point rods, signal wires and anything else that may have been in their way, to be first into the waiting motor coaches. The only successful way of collecting tickets was while the train was in motion, and even then there were difficulties.

At that time, Buckingham Station had good reason to boast of its flower gardens. It had a record of winning the LMS Station Garden Competition and there was much rivalry with certain other stations along the branch line. Harold Plant kept the gardens immaculate for many years until the line closed. He was a signalman and had to meet all trains as they arrived, to take or change the single-line staff. He was very much in contact with the passengers and many praised his garden. He would accept such compliments without revealing too much pleasure.

So one can imagine how Harold had no affection for high spirited schoolboys who disturbed the quiet of his country station, and who did not take life as seriously as himself. He was not a latter day Bigot of Buckingham but he was scornful of frivolity particularly when it occurred on his 'patch'. His annoyance can be visualised in an episode which occurred during the latter period of the Stowe School Vacation Specials. As the train slowly departed from Buckingham for Euston, one of the miscreants fired an air-gun at Harold's departing form while he was walking back to his signalbox. The shot missed, but Harold with a look of disdain said to those standing near *There goes a future prime minister of Britain'*. Harold's prophecy has so far not been realised, but the school has recently accepted a small number of girls so the chances of it happening may have been improved.

Buckingham Station.

The Fire at Moco Farm

Near to Swanbourne Station, approaching an up gradient from Winslow on the right hand side of the line, is an attractive pond which probably owes its existence to the original railway builders. Close by stands a farm which was once nearer to the line than it is today.

Moco Farm, spelt in various ways over the years, was farmed by the Heady family. Charlie Heady was the last of the Heady family to live there. He got to know many of the railwaymen who picked up his milk at the station, and who passed by on the trains. Charlie also learned of the crossing keeper's trick of getting a cheap supply of coal by putting a bottle or a scarecrow on the fence, knowing that the firemen on passing goods trains would try their luck at knocking it off with a lump of coal.

Before the Heady family worked the land, the farm was owned by Sir Thomas Freemantle. The original farm buildings

which stood close to the line had caught fire and burned to the ground, it was alleged that sparks from a particular engine had caused the fire; and Sir Thomas claimed damages against the LNWR. As a result, the village of Swanbourne came into the national news, probably for the first time. The incident also made prominent news in railway circles, and the ensuing court case provided an important precedent.

For some years previous to this incident various properties throughout England had been damaged by fire caused by sparks from passing engines, and considerable sums of money had been paid in compensation by the railway companies without recourse to legal action. In this case the LNWR decided to contest the claim, making it a test case in order that the legal position should be established once and for all. The point would be settled with certainty as to whether a railway company should be answerable for damages caused by their engines when travelling on the line. The company had taken every precaution that human skill could accomplish, not only in the daily operation but also in the design and construction of locomotives, availing themselves of every innovation that science and invention could suggest, in order to be as near perfect in every detail as possible.

The case was heard at Aylesbury Assizes, and the railway world held its breath. Sir Thomas Freemantle held that a spark from an engine passing along the line, had fallen on the thatched roof of one of his farm buildings, setting it alight and eventually burning it down. Therefore, it was argued, the company was guilty of negligence, through the carelessness of the driver, and liable to pay damages.

The case for the LNWR was that the engine was so constructed that if it did emit sparks they were innocuous, since they dispersed into the atmosphere and were extinguished before descending. Eminent engineers said that they had carefully examined the engine in question; it was of the highest standards of construction, and in good condition being almost new. Also, the Company had been granted powers, by Act of Parliament, to construct a railway; in turn they were compelled to provide a passenger and goods service at a quoted scale of fares and rates, and having fulfilled their obligations and taken every precaution with the design and service of their engines, they should have no further liabilities!

Mr. O'Malley QC, counsel for Sir Thomas Freemantle, cross-examined Mr. Fairburn, the Company's principal representative and an authority on such matters. His evidence was said to have been concise and conclusive. Finally Mr. O'Malley asked him 'Well sir, you mean to say that this engine was built with all the skill that human ingenuity could suggest?' 'Yes', was the confident reply. 'That it was impossible— absolutely impossible— for it to emit sparks that could burn down a building?' 'Yes', repeated Fairburn, 'except from the greatest carelessness on the part of the stoker.'

Mr. Fairburn had been very careless himself. The QC immediately turned to the judge: 'I submit my lord, that the evidence of the defendant's own witness fully establishes our case. If the jury is satisfied that these buildings were destroyed by a spark from the engine, it follows that there was great carelessness on the part of at least one of the servants of the defendant, and I therefore claim the verdict'. The learned judge summed up and the jury found in favour of the plaintiff.

J. Fowler in 'Echoes of Old County Life', comments that some weeks after the trial, he was in conversation with the Line's Locomotive Superintendent, who confided that although the Company's witnesses had been correct in asserting it was impossible for the engine to have caused the damage, the fire had in fact been started by another of the Company's engines which had gone up the line a few minutes earlier. He and some of the drivers had been aware of it throughout the trial. Presumably it might have been more difficult for the Company to prove in Court that that engine was so well constructed, and in such new condition.

Summing up the hearing J. Fowler aptly commented, 'The jury's verdict, as so often is the case, though wrong on the actual strict facts of the case before them, was just in substance!

Charlie Heady, the last of the family to live at Moco Farm adds a tailpiece to the story. Sadly, four horses died in the fire and were buried in the farm meadow. In the course of time their graves sank and for many years hollows marked their burial place. Now three pear trees are growing there.

Wolverton Bloomers

Wolverton was an important station on the London and Birmingham Railway. By 1844 Doctor Lipscomb, the historian, described it as a gigantic station where all trains stopped to change engines, and passengers obtained refreshments and used the lavatories. In 1846 it all became part of the London and North Western Railway. As engines increased in size and became capable of long journeys, so the station decreased in status. But the large engine sheds were still to have moments of glory.

J. E. McConnell Locomotive Superintendent at Wolverton designed and built simple, orthodox engines. When the LNWR announced their intention of running express trains between London and Birmingham in two hours, McConnell was ready to 'have a go'. He had a dashing sport-loving temperament which revelled in a challenge. From his early experience with the puny Bury engines, and Stephenson Patent long boilers, his own design of 'Bloomer' 2—2—2 was born. These 7 foot Bloomers were truly splendid engines but poor track prevented them showing their full capabilities.

They attracted the nickname 'Bloomer' after Amelia Bloomer, who designed some leg revealing clothes. McConnell's new express engine had also 'cleared away the decent skirting of an outside frame' and exhibited all the wheel to the traveller's gaze.

Feelings of contentious rivalry existed between Wolverton and Crewe. While McConnell was designing and manufacturing his Bloomers at Wolverton, the Northern Division was building Ramsbottom's own express design, the *Lady of the Lake* 7ft. 6in. single.

An Extra Large Bloomer.

McConnell's extra large Bloomer came out in 1861 and only three were built. The Marquis of Chandos was Chairman of the LNWR at the time, and McConnell knew he was safe from the antagonism of Richard Moon of Crewe whilst the Marquis remained in that office. Unfortunately the Marquis resigned that year, and Admiral Moorsom took over but died within the year, so Richard Moon became Chairman. There had long been conflict between McConnell and Moon and so, realising his position would soon be untenable, McConnell resigned.

This was just what Moon wanted. The Northern and Southern Divisions were amalgamated and Ramsbottom was appointed Chief Mechanical Engineer for the entire LNWR.

Less than a year after the merger, a political event of great importance brought both the locomotives into public eye. The performance of a Ramsbottom *Lady of the Lake* class, and a McConnell extra large Bloomer, became a focal point in a train journey of dramatic importance.

The two engines concerned had a contrasting outward appearance but were both of 2—2—2 wheel arrangement. The Lady was in plain dark green livery with single black lining whilst the Bloomer was painted in pillar-box red set off by flashing brass and copper work wherever a fitting existed.

During the American Civil War when the rebel states of the South were anxious to obtain diplomatic recognition, two prominent southerners sailed for Europe in the British merchant ship Trent. The Northern states got wind of the South's intention and, when 250 miles out from Havana, the Trent was fired on by an American warship and stopped. The delegates were taken from under the protection of the British Flag and into custody. Feeling in England naturally ran high and the government of the day delivered an ultimatum that, if its demands were refused, it was tantamount to a declaration of war. The weeks that elapsed before the reply came through was a time of intense excitement and the most careful preparations were made to convey the despatch to London as quickly as possible.

From 2nd January, 1862, Holyhead kept a first class express engine ready for instant departure toward London. It was not until 7th January, however, that the steamer carrying the Queen's messenger and the precious despatch came alongside the Admiralty pier at Holyhead. An old Allan single wheeler, No. 16 *Cerberus*, pulled the saloon carrying the messenger, round to the main station. There, a *Lady of the Lake* class No. 299 *Watt* was waiting to back on to the front van. Within minutes she was away, aiming to cover the 130½ miles to Stafford non-stop in 144 minutes, an average speed of 54.3 mph.

Great importance had been placed upon conveying the Queen's messenger from Holyhead to Euston in five hours from the moment of arrival of the steamer; that was a target speed of 52.7 mph overall. The newly installed water troughs near Aber enabled the first 130½ miles to be made non-stop.

The train ran past Stafford Station to Trent Valley Junction, half a mile to the south where engine changing could be more expeditiously arranged. There had been cross winds off the Irish Sea; in consequence the 59½ miles from Bangor to Chester took as much as 68½ minutes, an average speed of only 52.1 mph.

On arrival at Trent Valley Junction, *Watt* was uncoupled and ran ahead on to the Birmingham line. Waiting on the Trent Valley line was an extra large Bloomer No. 372. The whole operation was so smartly done that the special train was at rest for a mere 1½ minutes! Off went the Bloomer on the remaining 133.1 miles to Euston.

Fog was reported south of Kilsby Tunnel, and there were no water troughs on the Southern Division of the LNWR. With further to go than the Holyhead to Stafford section, the task set No. 372 was a stiff one. The first 49½ miles to the junction with the Birmingham line outside Rugby took 46½ minutes, a start to pass

117

average of 64 mph. Then the fog began to take its toll and the 50.9 miles from Rugby to Tring took 62 minutes. By Tring, however, they struck clear weather once again. By that time only 32 minutes were left to complete the journey. The driver gave the engine her head and the 29.3 miles from Tring to the north end of Primrose Hill Tunnel took 26 minutes, an average of 67.7 mph, and with time in hand the train coasted into Euston at 1.13 pm, two minutes inside the schedule.

The arrival at Euston had all the elements of drama. Before the train came to a standstill the Queen's messenger, carrying the precious despatches, had jumped from the saloon and was racing across to a waiting carriage. He was being driven through the main gates of the station toward Downing Street, as the Bloomer came finally to rest.

The credit for this locomotive's fine performance was McConnell's; whereas the Lady had averaged 57.2 mph, with water troughs, from Holyhead to Trent Valley Junction, the extra large Bloomer had run the 133.1 miles to Euston in 139½ minutes, an average of 57.2 mph without water troughs, ten minutes being lost because of fog. Had it not been for the weather between Rugby and Tring the journey from Trent Valley Junction to Euston would have been made in a record time for that period.

Because of Moon's attitude towards McConnell, the performance of the Bloomer was discreetly ignored.

Lady of the Lake: at the time of the story
its colour was green, but like all LNWR engines
it was subsequently painted black, during
the chairmanship of Richard Moon.

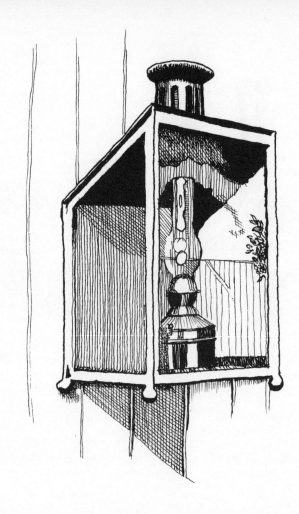

Tally-ho Hanmer

The railway history books contain numerous stories of landowners refusing to allow the railway to pass over their land. There are tales of hardship where farmers were not adequately compensated and there are tales of landowners who made more than a healthy profit. There were also cases of physical conflict, as in the case where the estate workers of the 1st Duke of Buckingham were instructed to put up all the obstacles they could muster to prevent the railway engineers obtaining levels when they secretly surveyed the land.

Simpson Parish Church

The story of 'Tally-ho-Hanmer', Simpson's wayward village parson, is about land sold to the London & Birmingham Railway Company for development, but it is a tale with a difference.

The parson rejoiced in the name of Tally-ho Hanmer because of his reputation as a keen and sometimes reckless huntsman. He was amiable to everyone but was seldom seen in any other costume than his riding boots with their mahogany coloured tops, and a square cut black riding coat, together with black breeches. On his head he wore a Jorrocks style low black hat with a broad, flat brim. But Tally-ho Hanmer was always short of money. With a garnished tale of distress he would frequently borrow a sovereign or a £5 note, from one old college friend or another. His tale was that he had sold some land he owned near Denbigh Hall and he was waiting for the money from the L & B Railway Company who were tardy in paying up.

On one occasion, a generous acquaintance feeling sympathy for the distressed cleric, forked out a £5 note to enable him to return home to his small Buckinghamshire Parish to take his Sunday Service. Soon afterwards however, the friendly sympathiser saw Parson Hanmer comfortably seated in an hostelry enjoying a good dinner and a bottle of champagne. But Tally-ho expertly talked his way out of a very awkward situation and wished his confused friend goodnight.

The borrowing continued, always with the promise that the loans would be refunded when he received his money from the L&B. But time was running out for Tally-ho. One less trusting creditor enquired at the Rugby offices of the Railway Company if the sale of land near Denbigh Hall had been settled. He discovered that the plausible vicar of Simpson had received the money long ago and had no doubt spent it all to maintain his far from pious way of life.

Tally-ho Hanmer was sent to a debtors prison, and even in there his plausible tongue enabled him to borrow £190 from a friend which he never repaid.

He was released from Aylesbury prison on 9th June, 1838 and managed to preach the good faith at Simpson Church from time to time. His rectory at Simpson was generally defended by a barricade, a protection against creditors throughout the week. Only on Sundays, when the law stipulated that a man could not be touched for debt, would he walk in his grounds and visit his parishioners.

Eventually he landed himself back in gaol, and he lost the living in 1850 when it was sequestrated to cover his debts.

It is said he died in Aylesbury Gaol, but whatever may have happened to him, he seems to have had an ignominious end for the younger son of the Lord of the Manor of Simpson.

Rough Justice

Many people now take for granted the procedures and safety regulations on our railways and forget that they were developed only after years of experience. The cost of that experience was paid for with the misfortunes and often the lives of many of the early railwaymen and travellers. Railway history shows that misfortune was dispensed not only by the hand of Fate, but also by the hand of Justice which was sometimes particularly rough.

One of the incidents that brought about a considerable improvement in railway signalling procedures occurred in 1847. It was paid for with the lives of seven people, injury to many others, and the punishment of the unfortunate Bernard Fossey.

Bernard Fossey was a railway policeman and the Blue Bridge, just south of Wolverton Station, was his signalling post on the night of 5th June 1847. The Euston Grove to Liverpool *night mail,* after a late start from Euston was approaching Wolverton on time. Driver William Manning had a white light on the front of his engine which denoted he was a passenger train. (The rules of 1847 required a green head light for a goods or coal train). When the *night mail* was about three quarters of a mile from Blue Bridge, William Manning could see a white light, presumably on a post near the bridge, which to him was an 'all clear' signal. However, about a hundred yards on the station side of the bridge, a pair of points led into sidings, and William Manning

The Blue Bridge near Wolverton Station.

could see a man running towards them carrying a green light. To the driver a green light meant caution, and should only have been used if he was a goods or coal train going into the sidings.

The man who was running with the green light was Constable Bernard Fossey who should have been carrying a white light to indicate to the driver that it was safe to enter the station.

The siding points were normally positioned straight for main line traffic; they could only be changed to allow a train into the sidings by a man holding them over, which took considerable care and effort. For some reason best known to Constable Fossey he held them over, directing the nineteen carriages of the *night mail* into the sidings. When driver Manning saw what was happening he immediately reversed his engine and sounded the whistle as long and as hard as possible to warn the two guards to apply their brakes. He soon found that a crash, with wagons already in the sidings, was inevitable and he decided to jump clear on to the embankment; an action repeated by his fireman.

The chief guard, William Cooper, was in his position on the roof of the rear van. He heard the engine's long whistle blast and applied his brakes as hard as he could but as the crash occurred he was thrown from his special seat, down the embankment. The under guard, Jacob Haines, also applied his brake. Somehow both escaped injury.

Despite the estimated speed of 10 miles per hour, the collision was violent and the carriages were driven back into each other. The two leading carriages were the Liverpool and Manchester Post Office parcel vans; the third and fourth were second class passenger carriages: these four suffered comparatively little damage. The fifth and sixth from the engine, two second class carriages, suffered most from the collision, one rising up on the other. Seven male passengers were killed in these carriages. Whilst the other carriages were little damaged several passengers received severe injuries.

It was a scene of chaos. Some passengers were seen rushing from the shattered carriages with blood streaming down their faces, whilst the severely injured, who could not extricate themselves, were heard groaning. But as soon as the wave of shock had passed, railwaymen and the more fortunate passengers came to the aid of the sufferers. Bodies were removed to one of the anterooms on Wolverton Station where the company's own surgeon, Mr. Rogers, and two other medical gentlemen, who were on the train at the time of the collision, were there to assist the injured.

Despite the chaos, death and injury, according to the *Bucks Herald* the mail train was detained only two hours. After the shattered carriages were removed from the line, the train proceeded on its journey. It was then that a special engine was despatched to London with a report for the general manager. The next morning Capt. Huish, Mr. Creed, and some directors arrived at Wolverton on a mail train to pursue an investigation.

Bernard Fossey was accused of the manslaughter of one of the passengers; the Coroner held him to account for the lives of the six others who were also killed. The case was heard at Aylesbury Assizes in September 1847, and reports of the hearing reveal a lot about working conditions and procedures on the railways at the time. It is significant now, over 130 years later, that nothing was offered in defence of the long hours worked in those days. Twelve hours, sixteen hours and sometimes more every day were quite normal and expected. In view of this the heavy responsibilities often placed on fatigued railwaymen were unreasonable, and as a result the dangers awaiting the early rail travellers were considerable.

When Bernard Fossey was questioned as to why he should give the 'all clear' signal to the approaching *night mail,* and then alter the points as though it was a goods train Fossey said that he had had second thoughts; he had suddenly doubted his initial identification, and believing it might instead be a goods train, he changed and held over the points for its safety. On hearing this the Superintendent of Wolverton Station gave him into the custody of William Smith Inspector of the Railway Police.

125

When the inspector was questioned by the judge, he explained that Fossey had been in service only six months but he had been properly instructed. He gave an account of Fossey's duties, which the court regarded as confusing; indeed the whole signalling system seemed far from clear, and it was obviously open to human error. But what was clear, was that Fossey should not have left his post: if he had stayed put, which was his instruction, he could not have altered the points. It was then revealed that another policeman should have been on duty at the Blue Bridge to signal the approach; he was away on some other duty and Fossey was standing in for him. Although it had to be admitted that poor Fossey's action had been confusing, it was little wonder, since the unfortunate man was attempting to do the two jobs at once.

It was here the judge expressed his disapproval of the Company for not keeping their servants properly posted. He put forward the view that the Company had too few hands to perform all necessary tasks. 'What is the use of signals if there is no one to attend to them?'.

The judge, summing up the evidence, told the jury the only question to be answered was whether the prisoner had, through carelessness and negligence, turned the train into the sidings. That he *had* was clear from his own admission. Could he then except by carelessness and negligence, have done so? He knew his duty and had been exercised in it; the distinction between the lights was sufficient to have enabled him to make out what his duty was. The light diffused around the train by the lamps in the carriages would alone suffice to show that the train was not for goods. It was evident that the prisoner expected a mail train and that no goods train was due at that time.

The jury had little choice but to return a verdict of 'guilty'; however, perhaps because of the cogent argument put up by a Mr. Prendergast in defence of Fossey, the jury added it was their opinion that the Company was also to blame for not keeping two men at the posts concerned. Although the blame was shared, it was only Fossey who was to be punished.

The judge expressed the view that the prisoner had been most properly convicted and, though of good character, he could do no other than inflict a severe sentence. The prisoner ought to have distinguished definitely between a goods and a passenger train; he had at first identified it correctly but subsequently changed his mind. If he had too much to do, he should have refused the duties imposed on him. The sentence of the Court was that he be imprisoned and kept to hard labour for a term of two years!

There was another accident in 1847, and this one may have helped improve work procedures in Loco sheds, although it would have been little consolation for the unfortunate Henry Elmes. He was a fireman at Wolverton, and like most firemen for the next 120 years, helped the driver oil the bearings and axleboxes of his engine. On a Wednesday morning in September at about 7.30am in Wolverton Loco Yard, Henry was carrying out the daily routine of preparing his engine (No. 48) for work. Behind the engine there were five others; steamraiser William Hayes was responsible for keeping steam in all the engines stabled in the yard. As he moved about his work he could see Henry oiling the axleboxes of his engine. To check if the axleboxes were clear of dirt and free of water it was necessary to put one's head through the wheel spokes to make an examination before oiling. Henry was in this dangerous position when driver Nevill on engine No. 13, which had just arrived at the yard from Rugby, was seen approaching. When the engines were about five yards apart, William Hayes, seeing the danger yelled at Elmes to look out, but he did not hear; moments later the locomotives collided. All the engines in that road were propelled backwards and Henry Elmes was killed.

Accounts of the evidence given by witnesses at the inquest provide us with a glimpse of Loco Shed practice in those days, and the lack of elementary precautions to prevent accidents.

It was usual practice for all drivers, when moving toward another engine on the depot sidings, to shout 'Look out'. The driver and fireman had the duty to see there was no obstruction or danger. In this case, driver Nevill and his fireman, John Lee, were both looking out the opposite side of the train from where Henry Elmes was working. Fireman Lee gave evidence that his driver did stop short, and shout 'Look out'.

Jonas Brown, fireman on another engine, and who was near by, said he had not heard Nevill shout.

The coroner said it was a question for the jury as to whether it was a case of manslaughter or an accident. He stated that both Nevill and Elmes were lawfully engaged in their work. Designed as the engine was, Elmes had no option but to put his head through the wheel spokes to see if filth had got into the axlebox as it did after every journey. The coroner said there had been some contradictory evidence.

The jury gave a unanimous verdict of 'accidental death', with a suggestion to Mr. O'Conner the LNWR representative, that if any improvement or regulation could be thought of and adopted to prevent a similar occurrence, they hoped the Company would not lose sight of it.

    There was another case of Rough Justice three years later. The punitive action this time was taken by the engine itself. A locomotive standing in the yard had been blowing off at the safety valves for some time. A labourer, thoroughly disliking the noise, silenced the engine by simply screwing down the safety valves. The constipated engine exploded, and a flying fragment sliced off one of his sensitive ears.

re-railing ramps.

Willy Wiggles in the Mess Room

The *history* of the railways is best learned from books, but there was no better place to learn about old railwaymen and legends of the country railways than in the Loco Mess Room.

In the early years of the second world war the oldest drivers had a railway career stretching back to the 1890s. When a number of them assembled in the mess room with their firemen and perhaps a few fitters and labourers from the yard, the discussion about some recent grouse or grumble would carry on until one could safely bet that some old sage would find a point in the discussion which would give him the cue to say, 'Now I remember in about 1906 when I was firing to old Bill Barden, we had a little DX and were coming up Ridgmont bank; the fire was completely buggered up and...' then it was time to sit and listen as some real history was unfolded.

Somehow the atmosphere of the mess room itself added to the story. The old, open fire grate was generally heaped with coal of which there was never any shortage. The red-hot mountain rose to a peak up the chimney, well out of view. A three gallon iron kettle would invariably be standing beside the fire, happily and incessantly steaming to provide continuous tea.

At Bletchley the mess room was attached to the engine shed. It was built at the beginning of the 20th century and it changed little in appearance throughout its life, excepting when the grime became so thick that paint and whitewash were a simpler choice than soap and water. Immersed as it was, in steam, smoke and coal dust throughout the year, every purging or periodic sprucing up was short lived, and the mess room quickly returned to the grimy state we all knew and loved.

The walls had no definable colour. I remember them only as dark, and timbered up to waist level. Wooden planks attached to the walls provided fixed seating and these, together ...

129

with two long well worn wooden tables and two high stools made up the furnishings. The iron framed windows were large, but because they were made of small frosted panes, cleaning was difficult and in any case a thankless task, and so the glass remained thickly grimed, which seemed to separate our society from the darkened world outside. Every decade or so the high ceiling beams were white washed. There was a yellow sink which was so chipped that its rough edge was used by fitters, labourers and enginemen to scrape the grease and file their callous hands. There was a perpetual smell of soap, and invariably in one corner of the sink, a small pile of sand was available to assist the process of beautification. Attached to the wall just inside the doorway, as though a reminder against carelessness at work, was an extra large ambulance box, high enough to hold a stretcher.

Through the eyes of a young cleaner, perhaps the oldest drivers would appear grumpy, ancient and formidable; but later his chance would come to reminisce, and viewing them in retrospect, although they might still seem ancient, they had about them a calm dependability which he could admire; a lifetime of conscientious service. With the passing of the years a story which once sounded simple and everyday, might later begin to give the listener a feeling of excitement and a sense of being connected with the past. Then eventually the young cleaner of yesteryear would become the old driver of today, and his stories of old railwaymen would be about another era. The pipe smoking old railwayman with the broad rural accent would tell stories not only of different scenery, and of different machines, but also of a different people. And the young, if they had the patience to listen, would sit wide-eyed and enthralled.

There was no more fitting place to listen to an episode of an engine failure, a rough trip with a badly steaming engine, skittles in the bar of the *Park Hotel*, or a much exaggerated story of some revered and long departed driver who once consumed an enormous amount of beer at one sitting: stories that would raise a laugh and give licence to others to tell similar tales, where perhaps 1905 seemed like yesterday to the Old, but like another world to the Young.

Apart from the age of particular occupants, a winters afternoon in the mess room in the 1950's would be little changed from a winter's afternoon some thirty years before. The onion peel on the table was the remains of the snap of a departed locoman. Fitter Ted Scott would have aired his grievance about the relative worth and rewards of fitter and driver. This would be followed by a short discussion on rules and regulations, and lead to an oft repeated anecdote about the badly steaming or overloaded engine. In easier years driver Freddy Eastaff would be sitting on the stool near the blazing fire, a shock of white hair beneath his shiny black hat. As he related his story with deliberation, he would be continually removing and replacing his pipe, and probably enriching his account of the little DX in years long past by exaggerating his rural Buckinghamshire accent. No sooner had he finished than driver Billy Stevens garnished the tale still further in a flurry of words that gave a clue to his nickname of Willy Wiggles. Willy talked and moved about, even on the footplate, like a jack-in-the-box. In the 1940s both Staffy and Willy Wiggles were approaching retirement, having been messroom characters for many years. Their old friend Packer Illing had also added considerable wit before he died some years earlier.

This same little group, plus a few others, might well have occupied the mess room on a Bank Holiday some 30 years before. Until the 1930s certain Bank Holidays were not granted to railway staff; they would have to book on duty like any other working day. But Bletchley, being mainly a freight depot, would have little for them to do. The foreman would possibly give some drivers the job of corking an engine, but generally much of the day would be spent in the mess room. Thus the day became one of long debates, stories, laughter and jokes. If Staffy had been in the working men's club and had a 'skin full' at lunch time, stories of past drinking deeds, or an account of a memorable game of skittles, would soon lead to him being induced to render a song. It would require little further persuasion to entice Willy Wiggles to accompany him in a duet and, perhaps from the table top, with Staffy's arm encircling Willy's shoulder we would be treated to an off-key rendering of, *Sweet Genevieve, I love the White Rose,* or *Springtime in the Rockies.* The two songsters would sing their hearts out, and tears would roll down their cheeks.

131

The mess room and the loco shed at Bletchley were demolished in about 1965, soon after the end of Steam. Their site is now the station car park, usually filled by 9.0 am with the cars of London commuters. The new Diesel and Electric Shed is situated on the opposite side of the main line. Its mess room has Formica topped tables, a gas cooker, and clear windows. Yellow fronted diesels and blue electric trains fill the shed. A new era in a vastly changed industry.

The Happy Go Lucky Line

It was four miles from Wolverton to Newport Pagnell along the single line railway. Overlooked by the windmill at Bradwell the line passed through a quiet rural backwater, twice crossing the Grand Union Canal, once near Wolverton, and again near a pub named the *Black Horse*. The bridge was the summit of a 1 in 80 gradient, and it often played a part in the incidents which make up the history of a pleasant, easy-going little line.

The Newport Pagnell line lived for 98 years; it was a 'family' branch, a line that belonged to the people of Newport Pagnell. There were mishaps galore, but somehow they were only ever minor, causing maybe temporary inconvenience or embarrassment; within days or even hours they left no more than a smile or a light hearted memory.

Only one engine was allowed on the line at one time, and this regulation had a lot to do with the quaint and winsome character that the line acquired over the years — earning it the affectionate title, *'The Happy-Go-Lucky Line'*.

The train 'staff' was issued at Wolverton No. 2 signalbox, and once 'Nobby', as the little train was often called, was in possession of the staff no other engine, in steam, could enter the line until the staff was returned to Wolverton. This regulation alone brought about many comic situations. The engine was stabled at Newport Pagnell in its own made-to-measure shed: it was 'king of the line', where no other engine could intrude. Its seclusion was jealously protected by those who served it, happy to remain out of sight, and hopefully out of mind, of 'big brothers' on the main line.

There was no signalbox at Newport. The guard or station staff worked the main points and signals from a ground frame, so that many of the usual rules and regulations did not apply. As a result mishaps occurred, but they were seldom serious. On rare occasions there were accidents which could not be covered up because the breakdown train had to be called out. On these occasions the chaps had to take their medicine. Whatever happened to Nobby the local passengers took it all in their stride, seldom if ever complaining however late the train arrived.

It all started in 1863. On 16th June, the Parish Church bells rang out to celebrate the passing of the Newport Pagnell Railway Act through the Committee Stage in the House of Commons. On 30th September 1865, the first engine hauling 17 wagons, crammed full with navvies went down the line. The next year the railway opened for goods, cattle and parcel traffic. Then on 2nd September 1867, there was the ceremonial opening of the line for passengers. It was a great day for Newport Pagnell which began with church bells ringing out as a Union Jack was hoisted from the tower. The streets were decorated, a large illuminated star hung from the *Swan Hotel* which also flew the Prince of Wales' feathers. There was a free trip to Wolverton at 1.15 pm and so many people turned up for the ride, hundreds had to be left behind on the platform. Champagne was served in the waiting room for railway officials and their friends. Rustic games and sporting events were held in Bury fields.

The Black Horse Inn, Great Linford.

The new line brought about the revival of the Newport Pagnell Steeplechase, and special trains were run to carry spectators.

The LNWR ran the line and employed an engine driver, a

134

fireman, and three permanent way men. The two intermediate stations of Bradwell and Linford each employed one man who, in his spare time, delivered parcels within a mile of his station. Other staff included the line manager, a guard, a porter, a goods foreman, a goods carman and three clerks, one for goods, one for booking and one general.

Driver Joseph Orchard was said to be the first LNWR driver on the line and he received 42/— per week, his fireman Benjamin Burbridge was paid 24/6. The permanent way men received between 17/— and 22/— per week, traffic men between 17/— and 27/—. The line manager was the only member of staff to live rent free and his salary was £12.10s 0d a month.

There was soon an announcement that it was proposed to extend the line to Olney. Plans were completed, the bridge over the Newport to Wolverton road was built, and much of the line was in the course of construction, when suddenly the project was abandoned.

In 1900 a spur was constructed off the line about a quarter of a mile from Wolverton Station, to connect with the up slow line. This formed an angle for turning the Royal Train coaches. But this introsion on Nobby's domain could be accomplished only when Nobby was at Wolverton and the train 'staff' could be borrowed. There was little change on the Happy-Go-Lucky Line from then until 1955, when the Newport Shed was closed and the engine crew supplied daily from Bletchley.

The sidings at Newport appeared as an extension beyond the platform reaching to the Newport— Wolverton road. There was a goods shed in the yard with the usual roads for coal and goods wagons. Shunting horses were used there until after World War II. The engine shed was a simple structure of wood and galvanised iron sheeting with sufficient room in front for coal storage. Just before entering the station a line went to Coles Mill. There was also a line parallel to the platform line which enabled the engine to run around the coaches and wagons. This line had a pair of trap points installed which, during a careless moment on the part of the driver, could derail the engine; although a ground signal was there as a reminder, it was known to happen.

Preliminary arrangements were completed in 1904 to electrify the line on the same system used by the Lancashire and Yorkshire Railway Company between Liverpool and Southport. Electrification seemed to promise considerable savings for the LNWR Board, but it did not materialise. It is hard now to imagine an

135

electrified Nobby.

Somehow the engine shed was burnt down on New Year's Day 1916, and a 4ft 6in Webb's tank engine No. 889 was so badly damaged it had to be dragged away to Crewe.

In the late 1920s the engine shed was damaged again, but not by fire. Just before departing with a 5.20 pm train from Newport to pick up the Wolverton workmen, Driver Albert Cox decided to take on more coal. The locomotive was uncoupled from its coaches in Newport Station and off it went to the shed. When the bunker was filled Albert took the engine back to the station to recouple it and to await porter guard Bill Beckett's signal to depart. During the usual chat with passengers, Bill overlooked his duty which was to reverse the points and lower the signal after the engine had returned. At 5.20 pm he waved for the train to depart and driver Albert, no doubt accustomed to seeing the signal left at danger, set off, he thought, for Wolverton. As the train veered off and passed the coal stage, Albert saw the shed looming close, but it was too late to worry. Through the shed and through the rear wall went engine and train, to rest peacefully, if heavily, in the ditch placed especially to catch runaway trains.

No one was hurt, but one lady passenger with eggs in her basket had a sticky mess to clear up. The shaken fireman, Les Lickorish, fortunately possessed a motor cycle so off he went to Wolverton, carrying the all important train staff, to get assistance. There on the crowded platform were the workmen, waiting and wondering what had happened to dear old Nobby. After a long delay, it somehow ended well. The day of reckoning had to come though, and Albert Cox got three days suspension as punishment. Bill Beckett waited with resignation for his turn. When the letter came for him to go and see the 'big chief' at Derby, his colleagues wished him good luck, and there was considerable conjecture as to what *his* punishment might be. It was a beaming Bill Beckett who returned to say he had been offered promotion, and was to become a passenger guard.

In those years the train would ply its way up and down the four miles of country branch line, well patronised by the local people. It was an institution of the town; it was there before most of the inhabitants were born, and there was no reason to believe that it would not remain there for ever more. At Bradwell Station there was a water column and at the end of each journey the locomotive was uncoupled to run round the train to return, taking water at Bradwell on the outward trip from Wolverton. At night the coaches would be stabled in the sidings, and the locomotive bedded down in the shed, complete with 'staff'. The line was locked up for the night.

In the mid-war years the line was supplied with LNWR tank engines fitted with a vacuum regulator on the smoke box side which enable the engine to push and pull a 'motor train'. The driver could sit in the leading coach driving compartment and, by various bell codes, instruct the fireman when to open or close the regulator.

The engine now sallied back and forth, pulling the train to Newport and pushing it back to Wolverton. Special regulations were enacted to allow Nobby to be a mixed train. Once a day, freight wagons would be attached to the rear of the passenger coaches.

There were now two drivers and two firemen stationed at Newport and everyone knew them, as they did also the guards and station staff. School children were regular travellers and they added their noise and laughter to the line.

It was about 1935 when a young cleaner from Bletchley, just passed to act as fireman, was sent to take the last train from Wolverton to Newport; he was to stay there overnight to be available to work the first train in the morning. He was young and had never been to Newport before. Les Measures,

Newport Pagnell Station, the end of the line. The little engine shed and coal stage referred to in the story are on the left of the single line.

taking compassion, pursuaded him to go home to Bletchley, and even lent him his own bicycle to do the journey, and return in time the next morning. However, the lad must have become disorientated by his unfamiliar excursions, and the following morning reported to Bletchley by mistake. Jimmy Palmer, the shift foreman, lost some of his calmness when he saw the lad walk in: 'Who worked the first passenger?' he asked with some excitement. The lad did not know but somehow the first passenger had run, and it was typical of the line that it had been accomplished without fuss.

The boy's name was Arthur Orchard, and he was grandson of Joseph Orchard, the first driver of the Newport Pagnell branch line.

For the next quarter of a century, the deeds of Nobby the Newport Flyer have become almost legendary.

To pull the Workmen's train up the heavy gradient out of Newport was as much as the diminutive tank engine could manage. In fact during the frosty weather, or when the autumn leaves were falling, it was often doubtful if the summit at Blackhorse bridge would be reached. On such mornings the fireman would

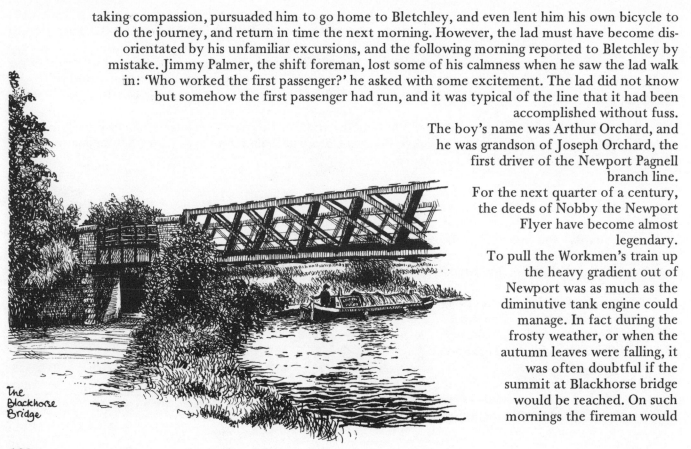

The Blackhorse Bridge

walk alongside the engine putting ash or sand on the line. Sometimes he would sand the rails for a considerable distance before starting. If they did come to a stand because of incessant slipping the driver would let the train run backwards, perhaps from a few yards off the summit, as far as Linford Station. They would get a good head of steam, then start again, belting the engine up the bank. Somehow Nobby always made it, even if it was half an hour late on arrival.

On one occasion Fred Baldwin could not make the summit and went through the procedure of running back. After carefully sanding the line he eventually made it but many Wolverton workmen were late for work. On the return journey that evening, Fred was presented with a small bag of sand, his name and a suitable remark attached.

The evening return of Wolverton's train was a very easy ride. The only problem was that the train was longer than the platform at Newport. It was common practice to unload the first coaches, then draw forward into the sidings. . . if the workmen would wait that long!

The Cole's Mill points at Newport Station were always laid for the platform or they should have been if the signal into the station was obeyed. There was an occasion during the blackout when the signal, as usual, was ignored. The points were set for Cole's Mill, and into the mill shot the crowded Workmen's train; it was only after great difficulty that the engine managed to push the heavy carriages out again since there was an even steeper gradient there then on the rise to Blackhorse Bridge.

During the war shed-labourer Joe Ashton worked regular nights unloading coal. Some of this fuel would be used for coaling the engine and keeping it in steam ready for the first train in the morning. Fred Baldwin knew that Joe moved the locomotive at about 2 am to a position where he could shovel coal into the bunker, so he put some detonators in front and behind the engine to give Joe a fright. As expected Joe moved the engine amidst successive bangs that echoed across the quiet, sleeping town. It is doubtful if the rapid explosions frightened Joe very much but soon through the darkness he could see, coming across the adjoining field, soldiers with rifles at the ready being deployed in a pincer movement around the engine shed. The explosions had awakened the Home Guard in their Headquarters at Major Cole's house. They were probably disappointed that Joe had nothing more lethal than a shovel!

There was another occasion when Fred Baldwin decided to make a noise. He was just about to leave with the 10 pm from Newport when he received a telephone message through the booking office that Mrs. Baldwin had been elected to the Newport Pagnell Urban District Council. Nobby departed from the station with the whistle blowing full blast all the way up the bank nearly to Linford and soon everyone in the town new the good news that Nobby had a relation on the council!

Joe Ashton was a handy sort of chap, or so fireman Fred Harris used to think. It was during the time of the motor train, when the trip from Newport to Wolverton would be made with the driver in his compartment at the front of the train and the fireman alone on the footplate of the engine at the rear. Fireman Fred used to do some evening courting at Newport between trips, but on one occasion he was late returning to his train and it had gone. Fred knew that Driver Timmy Orchard was not the sort of chap to go on his own, he also knew that a motor train was unlikely to complete the journey without a fireman. Fred got on his cycle and tore off to Wolverton. There he found Joe Ashton quietly filling the tank, and Timmy the driver quite unaware he had left his fireman behind. Evidently Joe was on the platform at Newport and had heard Timmy ringing for the fireman, and so he jumped onto the vacant footplate and off they went.

Joe would also help unofficially on other occasions. He would move the engine in the early hours of the morning to heat the train and give the early passengers a warmer ride.

Fred Baldwin was known to scatter corn on the railway, particularly where a poultry farm adjoined the line. With a little luck there might be a slight accident on the return trip and Nobby would arrive home with the Sunday dinner.

Over the years, many a fireman made himself at home in the booking office and forgot the fire of the engine outside the door. When it was time to depart it was all hands on deck to find wood to assist the few sparks that remained in the firebox . . . the passengers would sit and wait without complaint.

The most embarrassing incident, perhaps of all time, was on a dark, wet winter evening when Fred Baldwin and his fireman came out of the foreman's office at Wolverton to find the fire almost out and the steam pressure very low. The coal in the bunker was of the soft Welsh variety which was noted for being slow to ignite. With the blower valve hard on, and cords pulled on the train brake cylinders, Fred and his mate set off very slowly hoping they might be helped by the down gradient and that pressure might pick up later. But alas, at Bradwell, Nobby came gently to a halt, right out of steam; the fire was completely out. Len Ewins, the Wolverton station foreman, lived near the station and, as he sat with his wife listening to the wireless, there was a knock on the door. Len opened the door to see Fred Baldwin standing there, wet and bedraggled. "Hallo Fred, what's the matter?" asked the surprised Len Ewins. "Have you got such a thing as some dry wood and a match Len?" Nobby reached Newport, but how late? Memories don't seem to stretch back that far!

Apart from possessing the only intermediate siding on the line, Goodman's scrap yard, Bradwell also possessed a water column which was supplied by town water. There was an alternative but very slow supply at Wolverton. Over the years Bradwell expanded, and houses were built at what became Top End which was on higher level than the station and the rest of the village. When Nobby was taking water, the houses began to lose their supply. On Mondays, housewives had their weekly wash interrupted, and fists were often shaken at the engine crews. Soon instructions were given that no water should be taken at Bradwell on Mondays; the slow supply at Wolverton had to be used instead. As more houses came, so there was an increased demand on the water supply at Bradwell and even more houses were deprived of water through the week. Soon orders went out that no further water was to be taken at Bradwell and the column wheel was padlocked. Needless to say, someone found the key and water was taken discreetly from time to time.

Bradwell station and its high water tank were often the scene of a prank or two. It was the job of the porter to stand on the platform waiting for each train, and as the trains ran into the station firemen would sometimes spray him with water from the engine coal stacking pipe. Porter Merrivale had received several drenchings from one particular crew, so he obtained a bucket of the best from the station cess pool. He then climbed the high water-tower and waited for them to pass. The crew did not think of looking up until the thick bucket-load came down on them. Porter Merrivale made himself scarce for sometime.

Generally the older drivers and firemen had a compassionate and helpful attitude to youngsters who were starting their careers. During World War II, a cleaner, Albert Young, was sent for a week of night duty in the engine shed. Driver Cyril Holman was concerned whether he was able to do the job. 'Don't worry boy, he said, 'if you get into any difficulties come and wake me', Albert was young and very green. He could clean and coal the little tank engine, but he discovered the little tank engine, had leaking tubes and that was new to him. The engine got low on steam and the injectors would not work. Albert had to do something so off he went to Cyril Holman's house at 2.0 am. Without fuss he soon got Albert out of trouble, advised him on how to keep a bright fire when the tubes were leaking, and then returned uncomplaining to bed.

Cyril would often go to the shed on Sundays, in his own time, when the engine was without fire in it, and pack some glands, rather than the engine should go to Bletchley for repairs.

The immediate post war years saw little change in the line; it was still a pleasant corner of rural England. The Oakley Foxhounds still met at Linford and the Station Master of Newport was still being instructed to inform Nobby's driver to bring his train to a stand if he should see hounds in the vicinity of the line. Albert Wallace, the junior porter at Linford, paid an annual visit to Linford Manor to collect a mysterious sum of ten shillings owing to the railway company. His natural curiosity gained him the information that five shillings was related to the window of the manor overlooking the line, the other five being ground rent for a water pipe running under the railway.

Porter guard Jack Miller, at about this time, had the enterprising idea of bringing his shot gun to work, and from his brake van he might manage to topple a pheasant perched on the fence separating the squire's land from the railway. The squires bailiff reported Jack's activities to the Railway Company and Jack was dismissed, but true to the line's tradition of tolerance,

Bradwell Station.

he was later reinstated.

The Buckinghamshire Otter hounds of Great Linford have now passed into history. It was in the 1930s that the otterhounds were last seen being loaded into a hound van. The van was attached to a special coach as it waited in Linford Station. At Wolverton the coach and van were attached to the rear of an express destined for the West Country or Scotland.

The year 1948 was not only nationalisation year, but it was also the year Ernie Dodds arrived at Bletchley Loco Shed as its new 'gaffer'. Ernie had four other small sheds under his command, and it was his duty to visit each of them soon after he arrived. When he paid his first visit to Nobby's shed at Newport he wandered around it unrecognised. Fireman Steve Palmer was busy caring for his pigs on a plot of land which stretched down to the railway fence at the rear of the shed. Ernie, seeing Steve busy with the pigs, ventured: 'Nice pigs you have there!' Steve agreed with him and asked 'Do you keep pigs?' Ernie assured Steve that he knew very little about pigs for he was the new shed foreman at Bletchley. Steve suddenly felt uncomfortable. The fire underneath the cooking pig food obviously came from the coal stage on the railway side of the fence. Ernie did not hint that he had noticed anything. Looking back, it seems quite likely that he did; Ernie was a special-ist turning a blind eye.

If Steve took advantage of the coal so near at hand, nobody considered taking advantage of the bullion boxes that arrived, perhaps a week or more between each delivery. Two large boxes would arrive at Newport by train. They were inconspicuous other than being unusually heavy. They came by train to Wolverton and were transferred into Nobby's brake van, usually without a guard being present, before leaving for Newport where they were taken into the booking office to await collection by the bank. The contents could be identi-fied by a code which everyone knew. If the bullion arrived too late to catch Nobby it was stored in the booking office until next day. Albert the porter-cum-clerk could hardly be said to have guarded it with his life. He kept the booking office as an open house for all who desired to walk in.

The first significant change in Nobby's life came in 1955. The line had been under scrutiny by Manage-ment for some time, and the decision was made to close the engine shed at Newport and supply engine and locomen daily from Bletchley. The line carried on in much the same carefree way; the new enginemen were all charmed by their new way of life and soon conformed to the traditions and ways of Nobby and its friends. Some drivers became over-confident with the little train down the steep gradient from Blackhorse bridge and skidding through the station at Newport: more than one nearly came a cropper.

Driver Jack Simmonds was once taking the freight with a 2—6—4 tank engine, a large engine for thee Newport line; he was full of confidence, as he applied the brake. The wheels picked up, and silently the large engine slid its way down to the station without any sign of stopping. The platform line was clear. Through the station it slid, down towards the buffer stops near the Wolverton-Newport road. The stops got closer and closer. Then simultaneously, Jack and his fireman decided to bail out one each side. The train carried on to the bitter end, and the stops were pushed back violently several feet. It was a breakdown job, but surprisingly little damage was done to the engine.

Wolverton Station.

On another occasion Harold Dump-leton let his fireman drive Nobby. Autumn leaves were falling along the line and as he applied the brake the wheels picked up. Despite the sand valves being applied, and the brakes released and quickly re-applied, it failed and the train slid through the station and into the rear of the stabled Wolverton Workmen's carriages. There was only one passenger on the train. Mick Denton, the fireman, was off the engine and along the train in a flash, to help a very shaken lady down

144

to the ground. She did not complain; she just smiled and continued on her way to work.

Nick set off to Wolverton on a bicycle carrying the 'staff' to allow the breakdown train onto the line. It was an unfortunate accident which resulted in a two day suspension for Harold. It would have made things worse to have admitted that the fireman was driving.

It would be unfair of me not to mention one of my own transgressions when it was my turn for a week on Nobby.

Leaving Newport in the morning with the school train was always quite a happy time. There was much yelling and laughter and jockeying for seats, with doors opening and closing until departure. When we arrived at Linford more children got on, then slowly the train moved out of the station. Suddenly and abruptly it came to a halt with the engine still in the station and the carriages full of children pushed up the line a few yards amid high hedges and leafy overhanging trees. The vacuum regulator on the smoke box side had failed and the train would not move in either direction. This was no new failure, it had been experienced many times on the line and the coal pick was generally the answer to the problem. That day Nobby was obstinate. I decided to seek the advice of Bill Taylor, the mechanical foreman at Bletchley. This could only be done by telephoning from a call box in the village. Linford Station did not possess the luxury of a telephone. Bill's advice differed little from what I had already tried, so I returned to have another go. The children were having a riotous time and I could see that much of the foliage along the line was being pulled inside the carriages.

The Newport Station Master then arrived on his motor cycle. He had come to investigate our 'disappearance' as reported by the Wolverton signalman. He suggested that he should take the train staff to Wolverton to allow the shunting engine, on to the line to haul Nobby into Wolverton Station. He had only just disappeared from sight when my least persuasive effort worked and we were in business, Nobby moved with ease. David Lowe, the fireman, agreed that the staff would not reach Wolverton for several minutes, so a race was on to beat the motor-cycle. A blast on the whistle, all heads disappeared into the carriages, and Nobby made a sprightly getaway.

We had under estimated the speed of the Station Master's motor cycle. Nobby was chugging towards Bradwell Curve, with Wolverton Station almost in sight, when another engine came steaming to our assistance. Loud blasts on the whistle and both engines came quietly to a stand. The Midland Freight Four coupled up to the leading coach and within two minutes we were in Wolverton Station. A happy band of children were bounding up the stairs almost before the train had come to rest.

With a face that expressed great displeasure, Wolverton Station Master was there to greet the train's arrival. He knew that Nobby had moved without being in possession of the train staff. This was a crime without equal and there were threats of a report. If we had been hours late, or limped in damaged, that would have been all right; somehow it was Nobby's Prerogative. But to move without being in possession of the staff . . . never!

I awaited the day when I would have to toe the line, probably in front of the Locomotive Superintendent at Willesden or Crewe. I was assured that the crime had been reported. For reasons unknown the summons never came. It was an unsolved little mystery of the Happy-Go-Lucky Line.

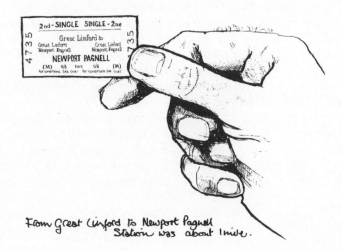

From Great Linford to Newport Pagnell
Station was about 1 mile.

Nobby was an institution that belonged to Newport Pagnell and the people were not willing to part with it without a fight. When proposals to close the line were announced there were many protesters. The Transport Users Consultative Committee heard objectors on 7th June, 1964; the enquiry incorporated the proposal to close Roade and Castlethorpe Stations just north of Wolverton on the main line. Despite the forceful arguments which were put up for the retention of Nobby and the Happy-Go-Luckly Line, it was scheduled to carry its last passenger on 5th September 1964. Newport Pagnell's one platform station was decorated with flags. Railway enthusiasts, and those who just wanted to be there for the last trip, waited for the 5.34 pm from Wolverton to arrive to make its final journey.

Arriving several minutes late, Nobby drew in to cheers. The 2—4—2 former LMS tank engine No. 1222 was photographed with enthusiasm as it had been on the Dunstable to Leighton Buzzard line when that line closed for passenger traffic. The Newport Pagnell and District Youth Clubs made sure that Nobby did not leave without full ceremony. Ralph Mazzone gave a cheerful imitation of Doctor Beeching and greeted all

Nobley.

the passengers. Other members of the club, dressed as cleaners and equipped with buckets of water, gave Nobby its final wash and brush up until one self-appointed cleaner gave 'Doctor Beeching' his just reward by tipping a bucket of water over his head.

Just after 6 o'clock the driver, Bill Faulkner received the 'right-away' signal from guard Albert Wallis and, amidst cheers and long blasts on the whistle, Nobby drew away whilst enthusiasts recorded the sounds of the wheels and chimney beat as it set out on its way to Wolverton. With crowds thronging the platforms at Linford and Bradwell Stations left behind to mourn its passing. Nobby's last run was slowly coming to an end.

A daily freight ran for a while and then . . . nothing. A ghostly avenue of trees and hedges remained after the track was lifted but new life was given to the line when tarmac was put down on the track bed; the former Newport Pagnell railway had become a public walkway to be enjoyed by the residents of the new city of Milton Keynes.

The Lampman's Hut.

Lampmen filled and changed the signal lamps; they would usually have their own huts where they could tend to the lamps and store paraffin. Signal lamps would often have to be carried long distances, and lampmen could be seen carrying yokes with several lamps on each side. They might sometimes receive a lift on the local goods engine: but it was no mean task to ascend the iron ladder of a signal post, carrying two lamps and exchanging them at the top for two others.

'The Lodge', Bletchley Station, with the trees
of Sir Herbert Leon's park in the background.
Until 1877 it was the office for the loco shed,
with the tank on top supplying water for the
engines. After, and right up until World War II,
it became the lodging house for enginemen
who were away from home for the night. It
contained 7 or 8 cubicles, with a bed and a
Bible in each. Residents were looked after by
a steward — usually a labourer from the
loco shed. He tended the gardens around
the Lodge, but during the war they deteriorated
and were eventually used to store old oil drums.
With the development of the station area, the
Lodge was demolished, but many of the trees
remain.

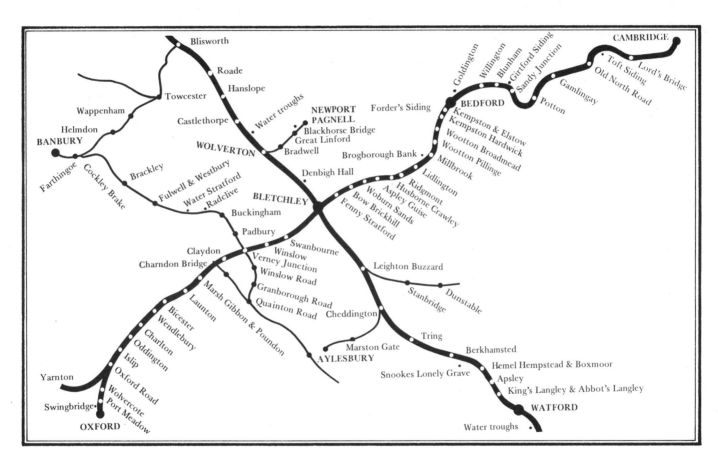

155